BIG BOSSES

BIG BOSSES

A Working Girl's Memoir
of Jazz Age America

ALTHEA MCDOWELL ALTEMUS

Edited and annotated by Robin F. Bachin

In partnership with
Vizcaya Museum and Gardens

THE UNIVERSITY OF CHICAGO PRESS

CHICAGO AND LONDON

The University of Chicago Press, Chicago 60637
The University of Chicago Press, Ltd., London
© 2016 by The University of Chicago

25 24 23 22 21 20 19 18 17 16   1 2 3 4 5

ISBN-13: 978-0-226-42359-3 (cloth)
ISBN-13: 978-0-226-42362-3 (paper)
ISBN-13: 978-0-226-42376-0 (e-book)
DOI: 10.7208/chicago/9780226423760.001.0001

Library of Congress Cataloging-in-Publication Data
Names: Altemus, Althea McDowell, 1885-1965, author. |
Bachin, Robin Faith, editor, writer of added commentary.
Title: Big Bosses : a working girl's memoir of Jazz Age
America / Althea McDowell Altemus ; edited and annotated by
Robin F. Bachin.
Description: Chicago : The University of Chicago Press,
2016. | "In partnership with Vizcaya Museum and Gardens." |
Includes bibliographical references.
Identifiers: LCCN 2016014271 | ISBN 9780226423593 (cloth :
alk. paper) | ISBN 9780226423623 (pbk. : alk. paper) | ISBN
9780226423760 (e-book)
Subjects: LCSH: Businessmen—United States. | Rich people—
United States. | Nineteen twenties. | Altemus, Althea
McDowell, 1885-1965. | Secretaries—United States—Biography.
| Working mothers—United States—Biography.
Classification: LCC HC102.5.A2 A58 2016 | DDC 651.3/741092—
dc23 LC record available at http://lccn.loc.gov/2016014271

CONTENTS

FOREWORD

"Big Bosses" is the memoir of professional secretary Althea
Maggie McDowell Altemus (1885–1965). Althea was born into
a family of factory workers in Woodstock, Illinois. She married
Wayne Altemus in 1910, and their son, Robert, was born in 1913.
After her husband developed an alcohol dependency, Althea divorced him in 1917. She furthered her career as a secretary in
the years that followed. Althea likely wrote "Big Bosses" in 1932,
when she was in her late forties, recounting details of her life
and her work as a single mother over the prior fifteen years. That
Althea created "Big Bosses" is extraordinary; that Vizcaya Museum and Gardens "rediscovered" the historically rich document
through Althea's grandsons was tremendously good fortune.

The typed manuscript runs nearly two hundred pages, con-
sisting of a preface and a dozen chapters. Each chapter poignantly describes an episode of Althea's life, with most organized around specific employment experiences. Her life is
largely typical for a working woman of the time, but it is exceptional with respect to the many internationally known figures
she encounters. The narrative begins in Miami, Florida, where
Althea moved in 1917 or 1918 to work as a private secretary for
International Harvester vice president James Deering at his
lavish and fantastical bayfront estate called Vizcaya (now the

The east facade of Vizcaya, James Deering's Miami estate, from Biscayne Bay, with the Barge in the foreground.

National Historic Landmark operating as Vizcaya Museum and Gardens). "Big Bosses" then follows Althea to Chicago, to her family's hometown of Elgin, Illinois, and then to New York. In each location Althea describes her quest for companionship and employment while maintaining a deep commitment to caring for her young son.

After working for Deering at Vizcaya, Althea apparently worked for such prominent business leaders as Samuel Insull, president of Chicago Edison; New York banker S. W. Straus; and real estate developer Fred F. French. She held less conventional positions, too, with a dissolute Swiss architect, the jealous wife of a "big boss," and a jeweler who catered to prostitutes. In the course of her work and travels, Althea also apparently encountered orator and politician William Jennings Bryan, inventor Thomas Edison, art patron Helen Clay Frick, and several actresses, including Constance Talmadge, who even cast Altemus

Still from the 1921 film *Lessons in Love,* with Constance Talmadge
on a bench in the foreground and (presumably) Althea Altemus at the
center of the circular table in the background, wearing a white tam-
o'-shanter. Image courtesy of Cohen Film Collection LLC.

as an extra in a Hollywood film. At the conclusion of "Big
Bosses," Althea describes her return to Miami during the 1920s
real estate boom and the tumultuous years that followed.

The manuscript is greatly enriched by Althea's inclusion of
twenty ink illustrations by architect Phineas Paist (1873–1937).
Paist was born and classically trained in Philadelphia, and he
studied abroad. He relocated to Miami in 1916 to work on the
Vizcaya estate, and he remained in the area thereafter, assum-
ing a leading role in the design of the city of Coral Gables. His
illustrations for "Big Bosses" were drawn on paper the same size
as the text pages and inserted where appropriate. All but one of
the illustrations represent characters or literal scenes from the
manuscript, with five featuring or including Althea's son, Robert,

referred to as "Tidbits." Each illustration includes a handwritten title or other identifying notation, and virtually all are marked with a number that is, likewise, referenced in the text. Paist's drawings are insightful and playful, complementing the content and tone of the narrative.

"Big Bosses" is at once personal and professional, candid and discreet. Althea created her memoir using a typewriter, the principal tool of her trade. Reading the original manuscript as a thick stack of 8-1/2″ by 11″ pages, with double-spaced text in traditional Courier font, one can imagine the staccato rhythm of Althea's fingers pressing the keys and the keys, in turn, striking the paper. And one can appreciate the immense effort it took to prepare "Big Bosses." (See figures on pages xvii–xx.) Althea's act of committing her tell-all tale to paper in so formal a manner seems extremely courageous, especially when one considers that she wrote "Big Bosses" without formal literary training and in a day devoid of correction fluid. That the resultant narrative is compelling, humorous, and insightful is impressive and moving.

Althea conveys the triumphs and hardships of her life as a single working mother in the early twentieth century, and she shares frank stories of the characters she encounters—her companions and her employers who range from ethical and loyal to unscrupulous and self-serving. Althea originally identified herself on the cover page of the manuscript as "A Private Secretary," only adding her name in handwritten notes after its completion. (See figure on page xvii.) She maintained in her preface that "Big Bosses" was based on actual facts, with the exception of names. Archival research suggests that some elements of the manuscript, indeed, adhere very closely to fact, while others are embellishments or fabrications. When typing the manuscript, Althea, in fact, used both actual and fictitious names; but at some point thereafter she apparently had second thoughts over the extent of her transparency and boldly, and perhaps hastily, used a pen to cross out some of the actual names in her neatly typed manuscript and replace them with handwritten pseudonyms. (See figures on pages xix and xx.) She also fictionalized her account by changing dates, conceivably making it more difficult to discover her identity in the event "Big Bosses" was published. It's unclear whether Althea wrote the manuscript primarily for personal reasons as a cathartic diary, or whether she actually hoped to publish it during her lifetime—sharing with all the world the extraordinary and sometimes unfortunate people and circumstances that shaped her life.

It is Althea Altemus's connections to Miami, in general, and Vizcaya, in particular, that led to the rediscovery, investigation, and publication of "Big Bosses." Althea retired in Miami, and her son, Robert MacDowell Altemus, raised his two sons, Robert and Donald, in South Florida. One day in mid-2012, I had the great luck of being introduced to Don Altemus at the Vizcaya Café and Shop by its gracious proprietor, Joy Wallace. Don enthusiastically informed me that his grandmother had been James Deering's secretary at Vizcaya. He also recalled that she had written a manuscript about her career, replete with compromising tales about her employers. By the summer of 2012, Don's brother, Robert, along with his wife, Tanya Lewicki, had located the "Big Bosses" manuscript deep in one of their closets. That August, my colleagues and I met with Robert and Don Altemus and gazed with wonderment at the manuscript, which appeared to be a kind of Rosetta Stone in our efforts to understand more about bachelor James Deering's life at Vizcaya.

Although Vizcaya's archives contain thousands of original architectural drawings of and correspondence about the estate's design and construction, documentation of how and with whom Deering enjoyed his winter home has been woefully scarce. There has been much speculation about Deering's interests and passions, and while "Big Bosses" leaves open as many questions as it answers, it was immediately apparent that the manuscript provided unprecedented insight into life at Vizcaya. Althea's narrative compellingly links and gives meaning to disparate facts scattered throughout dozens of archival documents. Each fact that we verified gave us greater confidence that "Big Bosses" could be viewed as a substantially reliable account of Deering, his habits, and his emotions. These include tales of how Deering smuggled liquor into Vizcaya during the Prohibition years; of the hospitality he extended to guests, including the invitation to boating and airplane tours; and of the loneliness and fear of his privileged but highly scrutinized life. "Big Bosses" has, in short, enabled Vizcaya Museum and Gardens to develop and share a much richer account of its history.

While the subjects of only a single chapter ("Wealth"), James Deering and Vizcaya played a central role in Althea's life and memoir. This is first evidenced by the handwritten list of Vizcaya personnel that appears near the front of the manuscript. (See figure on page 8.) The list seems to reflect the fact that Althea worked at Vizcaya at the pivotal moment in which James Deering had begun to occupy the estate though it was still being completed, for it includes both design and operations professionals. In an order that is either random or highly personal, Althea identifies Vizcaya's architects, accountants, secretaries (listing herself), the bookkeeper and accountant (again listing herself), decorators, superintendents, and the gardener.

The ink drawings by Phineas Paist also reflect the author's

close connections with Vizcaya. Althea presumably met Paist while they both were working for Deering, and they apparently maintained a relationship over the years. Paist's illustrations for "Big Bosses" pay special attention to Deering and Vizcaya. While many of the drawings in "Big Bosses" depict a single character with little or no context, several of Paist's Vizcaya illustrations represent two characters in architecturally identifiable contexts, including one depiction of Althea at her desk while Deering is running frantically toward his bathroom and another showing John Singer Sargent painting Deering's portrait in Vizcaya's bay-front East Loggia. Clearly Paist was most familiar with and enthusiastic about the Vizcaya topics in "Big Bosses," making his drawings useful educational tools.

Finally, it was enlightening and touching to read Althea's fond recollections of James Deering and Vizcaya throughout "Big Bosses." Althea conjures Deering as a former employer whom other "big bosses" know and respect; she remembers Vizcaya as a paradise characterized by "foreigness [sic], friendliness, beauty and happiness"; and she learns from a friend who met Deering in Paris years later "that he was sorry [she] had deserted him." Deering and Vizcaya recur as positive memories for Althea throughout "Big Bosses" and stand in stark contrast to some of the less scrupulous people and contexts she later encountered.

Notwithstanding the Vizcaya connection, it was also immediately evident to us that "Big Bosses" had far-reaching sociohistorical relevance as the first-person account of a single working mother in early twentieth-century America. Althea reveals in a very personal way the discriminatory hiring practices that women, especially mothers, faced. And she recounts the increasing freedom and independence that wage-earning women experienced by the 1920s. We recognized that "Big Bosses" could enlighten and entertain general audiences as well as those interested in gender, labor, business, and urban history, and so we set out to publish it.

In September 2012, Althea's grandsons, Robert and Don, generously donated the manuscript to Vizcaya Museum and Gardens, and we committed to researching and disseminating the details and broader context of their grandmother's life and work. I had no doubt that University of Miami historian Dr. Robin Bachin was the ideal choice for such task, given her interests in women's labor history and in Miami and Chicago, the cities in which most of "Big Bosses" is set. Robin's annotations and afterword shed great light on Althea and the world in which she lived. Unfortunately, Robert Altemus passed away before this project was completed, but his brother, Don, and his wife, Tanya, have both provided important materials and information for this publication. And so we dedicate this publication to Althea Altemus, her son, Robert, his sons Robert and Donald, and their families.

Dr. Joel M. Hoffman
Executive Director
Vizcaya Museum and Gardens

SAMPLE PAGES FROM
ALTHEA ALTEMUS'S
ORIGINAL MANUSCRIPT

B I G

B O S S E S

BY
A PRIVATE SECRETARY

WEALTH

Neither beautiful nor dumb I had received my first assignment as private secretary to probably the world's oldest and wealthiest bachelor playboy.

With the mature judgment of twenty lovely summers and fewer winters, fortune had come my way following three years of the now elapsed matrimony which bequeathed unto me a tiny liability of the stronger sex. It was 1922, America had been at war, money was tight, work was scarce, and years loomed ahead in which to furnish the wherewithall for cute little Tidbits.

I wasn't hard to look at, i.e. if you didn't look too hard, and here was opportunity as secretary to the Ex-President of Teaser and Reaper, Inc.

Now this big boss had retired from active work and although his past was rumored as a panorama of living dramas, comedies and what-have-you, nevertheless he had decided to gracefully and quietly drift into the decrepit years, peacefully alone in a seven million dollar villa not far from

Phylander

~~PYNCHON~~ & COMPANY

My next engagement was a long and happy
one as secretary to a partner of ~~Pynchon~~ & _Phylander_
Company, members of the Chicago Board of Trade.

It was nice to be in real business
and my "Big Boss" here was one of the grandest
men I have ever known - young, handsome,
pleasant, practical but with an appreciation
of beauty, kindly and generous. He had only
one hobby, and whether stocks were selling
long or short, golf took precedent. I told
him of Tidbits as he appeared so genuinely
human, and he was one of the few real executives
I have met who was big enough to think it
possible for a clever and capable secretary
to be also a mother.

The work with this Company was very
interesting, buying and selling stocks and
bonds. The hours were short - nine until
two - and what a treat it was to do a day's
work and be home for a hour or two with the
children before dinner time. Blossom was still
with us but now that generous monthly checks

134

from tears and he appeared a complete
physical wreck. If ever a man needed
a bracer now was the time, but outside
of pencils, poems and forgetfulness he
had no bad habits. He told me how his
young wife had left him, leaving at
home their year old baby. She had removed
all negotiable securities from their
safety deposit box, drawn all funds from
checking accounts, bought a brand new
roadster on his credit and had disappeared.

After a nervous breakdown this
splendid Chief did not have the inspiration
to promote more clubs, and as his mental anguish
worried me too much, I resigned.

****

Before answering advertisements
or visiting agencies relative to a new
business connection, I decided to write
to ~~Henry Clay Frick's~~ Envry Kay Hicks daughter ~~Helen~~ Ellen,
who was noted for her charities and
benevolence. Her mother's brother was
my husband's uncle and he had lived with

152

A NOTE ON THE TRANSCRIPTION

Big Bosses faithfully replicates the text of Althea Altemus's original typed manuscript, though some minor corrections have been made throughout: spacing between words; obvious punctuation errors; and mistyped, duplicated, or omitted words. Some hyphenation has also been adjusted to contemporary standards. Three words now viewed as pejorative have been eliminated.

However, misspelled words, grammatical irregularities, and formatting inconsistencies have all been retained to reflect the challenges Altemus faced in writing a manuscript of this length, sophistication, and complexity on a typewriter, as well as her limited education and training.

The footnotes throughout the manuscript are not original. They were added to provide readers with important background information. The "Historical Annotations" following the afterword present in-depth research on the subjects discussed by Althea Altemus. These are organized by manuscript page number, with each note introduced by the passage to which it relates.

To invoke the character of Altemus's typewritten document, the Courier font is used for her original chapter titles and narrative conversations, and for the above-referenced footnotes.

32,000 words
Mrs. Althea Altemus
63 S.E. 6th St.
Miami, Florida.

B I G

B O S S E S

BY

A   PRIVATE   SECRETARY

CHAPTERS

* In the first of several manual edits to the typed manuscript, Altemus handwrote the fictitious name "Phylander" over the actual name "Pynchon."
† This chapter title did not appear in the original table of contents.

(Sketch A)

PREFACE

A STORY OF ACTUAL HAPPENINGS

With the exception of names, which are mostly fictitious, these few chapters portray incidents in the life of a private secretary, viz. the authoress, who at twenty years of age was left a widow with infant son.[*]

Rather than assistance from either parents, or parents-in-law, she chose a business career and independence, and it is hoped that the following resume of her adventures, friendships, laughter and heartaches, during the successive ten years, may be of interest to readers of this booklet.

(Sketch B)

---

[*] Althea Maggie (Marie) McDowell (MacDowell) Altemus, was born on December 4, 1885, in Woodstock, Illinois. Throughout the manuscript, the dates of events and ages Althea cites for herself are inconsistent or wrong (e.g., she was twenty-seven when her son, Robert MacDowell Altemus, was born, and she and her husband, Wayne Hughes Altemus, divorced in 1917, several years before his death). So, too, are some of the stories she tells. At various times in her life, Althea used her married name and at others her maiden name, even after marriage. Since she used the name Althea Altemus for the authorship of the manuscript, she is referred to as "Altemus" throughout the text. See the afterword for further discussion of Altemus's life, family, and work.

*All drawings in this book by
Phineas E. Paist, Arch etc Viscaya
Supervising Arch Coral Gables Fla 1925-1930
         "   "   City Hall
         "   Miami Post office
Artist - Paris, N.Y. Miami.**

1922

1923

Tid-Bits

SKETCHES A AND B†

* Phineas E. Paist (1873-1937) was an on-site project architect for
James Deering's Miami estate, Vizcaya. A noted artist and architect,
he also helped design the new city of Coral Gables in the 1920s as
lead colorist, supervising the choice of colors that shaped its Mediterranean aesthetic.
† Robert Altemus, referred to as "Tidbits" in the manuscript, was
born in 1913, so in 1922 and 1923 he was older than he appears in
sketches A and B.

*Architects of Viscaya**
  F. Burral Hoffman N.Y.
  Paul Chalfin   "
  Associate Arch. Phineas Paist N.Y.

Accountants - Viscaya
  Haskell & Sells - Chicago
  Miami Corporation - "

Secretaries - Viscaya
  Mary Northwood Chicago
  A MacDowell Altemus "   & Miami
  Roger Conant Miami & N.Y.

Bookkeeper & Acct. at Viscaya
  1916 - 1923
  A MacDowell Altemus

Decorator - Interior at Viscaya
  Phineas E Paist
  Paul Chalfin
  Elsie de Wolfe (occasionally)
  Bob Chandler N.Y.

Superintendents Viscaya
  Mr. Sturrock
  "   McGinnis

Gardener - Alec Donn – Exotic Gardens

* Vizcaya was the Miami estate of American businessman James Deering, and the first place of employment Althea Altemus describes in "Big Bosses." Altemus included a handwritten list of Vizcaya's design and operations personnel on the verso of the table of contents in the original manuscript. (See figure on page 8.) It has been transcribed verbatim with errors.

Architect of Vizcaya
   J Burral Hoffman N.Y.
Paul Chalfin   "
Associate Arch. Phineas Faist N.Y.

Accountants – Vizcaya
   Haskell & Sells – Chicago
   Miami Corporation –   "

Secretaries – Vizcaya
   Mary Northwood Chicago
   A Marckwald Attenus   " + Miami
   Roger Conant Miami N.Y.

Bookkeeper & Acct. at Vizcaya
      1916 – 1923
   A Marckwald Attenus

Decorator – Interior at Vizcaya
   Phineas E Faist
   Paul Chalfin
   Elsie de Wolfe (occasionally)
   Bob Chandler . N.Y.

Superintendent of Vizcaya
   M. Stukerck
      " McGuire
Gardener Alec Donn Exotic Gardens

WEALTH

Neither beautiful nor dumb I had received my first assignment as private secretary to probably the world's oldest and wealthiest bachelor playboy.

With the mature judgment of twenty lovely summers and fewer winters, fortune had come my way following three years of the now elapsed matrimony which bequeathed unto me a tiny liability of the stronger sex. It was 1922, America had been at war, money was tight, work was scarce, and years loomed ahead in which to furnish the wherewithall for cute little Tidbits.*

I wasn't hard to look at, i.e. if you didn't look too hard, and here was opportunity as secretary to the Ex-President of Teaser and Reaper, Inc.†

Now this big boss had retired from active work and although his past was rumored as a panorama of living dramas, comedies and what-have-you, nevertheless he had decided to gracefully

---

* Althea here implies she is a divorcée, not a widow, as she did in the preface. While she says the year is 1922, she moved to Miami in late 1917 or early 1918.
† "Teaser and Reaper" here stands in for the International Harvester Company, formed after the merger of the McCormick Harvesting Machine Company and the Deering Harvester Company, the largest manufacturers of agricultural implements in the nation. This "big boss" is James Deering.

and quietly drift into the decrepit years, peacefully alone in a seven million dollar villa not far from Palm Beach, with only a couple hundred servants, three yachts, four cruisers and a few other necessities of modern comfort.*

First I must tell you that he was a Beau Brummell of three score and ten, tall and distinguished, always perfectly groomed and a patron of art and French classics. In fact he adored anything and everything French.

His salon was Louis XIVth, his bedchamber Louis XVth, his bath an embroidered tent ala Louis XVIth, and his sleeping couch a copy of Napoleon's from the Petit Trianon.

To describe his villa, Eden, would only bore you with its voluminous detail.† Enough to say that the greatest talent and genius of the day had been commissioned to bring to reality on the beautiful shores of Biscayne Bay the atmosphere of old world culture and art. It had taken five years to build this estate and though occupied was still incomplete.

My duties started at 10 A.M.

(Sketch 1)‡

* Altemus refers to Vizcaya, James Deering's lavish winter estate in Miami, where she worked as his private secretary. In reality, the staff likely numbered closer to fifty, and Deering was fifty-seven or fifty-eight when Altemus began working for him.
† "Eden" refers to Vizcaya.
‡ This is Paist's most complex image, showing Althea Altemus at a desk in Deering's sitting room on the left, Deering running in a robe through his dressing room at center, toward his lavish bathroom at right. Although eliminating the bedroom between the dressing room and the bathroom, the drawing accurately captures the connectivity among the suite of rooms, the medallion in the sitting room ceiling, the desks that accommodated Deering and his secretary, and the general configuration of the bathroom, including the placement of Deering's shaving stand overlooking the bay.

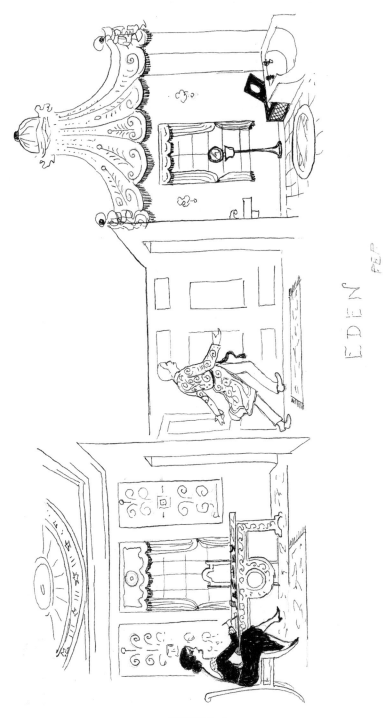

SKETCH 1

Beau, we'll call him for short, was very prompt in all things, and after a plunge in the marble and gold pool - in his embroidered tent - and a hearty breakfast of calomel and seltzer, was always on the job promptly at ten.*

Five minutes were alloted to sort the mail - five groups in all - business, social, love, foreign and miscellaneous.

Most important were the dear messages of love and passion. This group was always a delight to me with its dainty envelopes of violet and jade, lovely pastel yellows, shell pinks, baby blues, now and then a grey and always a white. Delicate lilac to sensuous scents of the Orient wafted from this group.

Only the lonely white missive seemed to be in a world apart, as Beau always picked up this precious document first. It did not take me long to know that this white message, with its strange scrawl, was not for even a secretary's eye to gaze upon. My youthful training warned me that curiosity killed the cat but I wondered what made the cat curious and intended to find out. One day I peeked over Beau's shoulder and there was that adorable phrase on the white note "With all my love, Nan". That little white envelope arrived every morning for several years and was never answered in my presence - it found a resting place in an inside pocket of Beau's beautifully embroidered waistcoat.†

---

* The "embroidered tent" is a reference to the ceiling canopy in Deering's bathroom, which had an elaborate bathtub. "Calomel" is a likely toxic compound of mercury that was prescribed for a number of ailments, including constipation.
† "Nan" most likely was Anne Odell (Winston), with whom Deering was rumored to be having an affair. Odell (or O'Dell) was the wife of Deering's friend Bertram McIntosh Winston, director of the Chicago Real Estate Board. Deering socialized regularly with the Winstons in Europe, and he kept two monkeys at Vizcaya named after them. At Vizcaya, the Winstons stayed for weeks at a time in the Galleon/ Caravel Suite, which connected to another guest room, Espagnolette, that had a secret door connected to Deering's bedroom via a balcony behind his bathroom. The connections among Deering's other private

With love letters out of the way, and calomel in the way, Beau would rush into his embroidered tent, thus giving me time to enjoy the dear little picture postals just in from Paris.

Next came the daily requests for money, arriving all the way from the far east to the golden west, and varied in sums from ten to a hundred dollars. These were sent by colored preachers, misunderstood wives, students, doll-babies in need of operations, cripples, the aged and infirm, schoolmarms, nurses, waitresses and any others you can think of. These letters we answered with a "nay" except the colored pastors, they always received a check.

The higher requests for loans of five hundred to a hundred thousand arrived mostly from France, the elite and the theatrical contingent of our country; huge amounts were necessary to finance coming out parties of debs, whose parents had probably met Beau somewhere and inasmuch as he was a bachelor they thought he would be delighted to furnish the funds for such a worthy cause. Even a former Director of Teaser and Reaper, Inc. needed one hundred grand and got it.

Invitations came in for third inspection. These were easy inasmuch as Beau had experienced and tired of all the thrills of modern society. The slim and stupid debutante failed to register, dyed in the wool phrases of the fat and forty madame were lost completely, and the repartee and allure of the charmer were just so much time wasted.

(Sketch 2)

We had stock regrets always on file and for the soirees of the Palm Beach group we sent replies of ten words - no more no

rooms are shown in sketch 1. According to Paul Chalfin, Bertram was "either a stupid man or a *mari complaisant*."

BEAU

SKETCH 2

less - "So sorry, but I have lost the effervescence of youth" - a plausible excuse, n'cest pas?

By this time it was most necessary that Beau make another dash for his Luis XVIth, after which the valet would serve several little nips of Chapin & Gore and then we were ready to take up the business of the day.*

Appointments with House Manager, Captains, Architects and Artists, Lawyers, Professors, Organists, Golf Pros and others, at fifteen minute intervals kept us busy until luncheon.

Our House Manager, according to her opinion was the only remaining descendant of the Mayflower, and any other pretenders should immediately be exterminated. Her Englishlike abhorrence of any tendency to earn one's living must have caused her real pain when obliged to spend a few minutes daily at the arduous task of O.K.'ing a few bills.

To her the entire place and contents were bourgeois and really to speak to this lofty dowager was a favor one could not forget. She came, she saw, but she didn't conquer because her reports were firstly nonplus, secondly non-legible and thirdly only once-in-a-while. She didn't make good with Beau and we were all happy to have her depart for wherever she came from.

Architects and artists were still engaged putting the final touches to this gorgeous Eden. They came from everywhere - some appeared in Fiats with Chow dogs, blue denim pants and apricot sashes - others with great flopping Panamas and goatees came in Fords or on bicycles. All had work to do at this unfinished Paradise. One very ladylike old dear lived in a houseboat -

* Altemus is referring to Chapin and Gore Old Reserve Bourbon Whiskey. According to Paul Chalfin, "Deering always had in one hand a tiny glass of whiskey and in the other a cigaret [sic], sipping first from one and puffing from the other."

which he called the Blue Pup - with his boy friend and Chows. Beau's sheckles financed for two years these dear boys during their sojourn to bring aesthetics to our country seat. And if you don't think the parties given on the Blue Pup were unique, ask the actress I am sketching herewith, for believe me she knows.*

(Sketch 3)

* *

Now Beau thought Eden wouldn't be complete without at least one decoration by the great and famous "Who's Looney Now", so along came this monstrous goof and enjoyed himself immensely for a couple of months.

If he didn't happen to be rhapsodizing with four or five native beauties he had sent over from Cuba, he could usually be found up in the towers sleeping with the peacocks he would inveigle up the winding stairway.

Beau asked Bob one day about his ten day marriage with the gorgeous Lina, and Husky replied "It cost me a million but it was worth it".†

* *

* Altemus here refers to Paul Chalfin's seventy-four-foot houseboat, the *Blue Dog*, whose parties regularly appeared in the *Miami Herald* society pages, as well as in the July 1917 issue of *Vanity Fair*. Based on the inclusion of a calla lily and the subject's appearance, sketch 3 likely depicts Lillian Gish (1893-1993), the silent film actress, who visited Vizcaya.

† "Who's Looney Now" is noted New York artist Robert Winthrop Chanler (1872-1930), known for his eccentric behavior. Chanler's brother, John, whom his family labeled insane, sent a telegram to Robert on the occasion of his marriage to opera star Lina Cavalieri and asked, "Who's Looney Now?"

SKETCH 3

Just about this time we had an uninvited actress visitor from New York. She was a lovely blonde with a peaches and cream complexion and a slight lisp. She announced herself - Mary Davis.*

Mary arrived sans baggage and thought it would be nice to spend sometime in this Eden. She told the butler she had just left Palm Beach where she received a ten thousand dollar diamond ring and he told her he hoped her present visit would be equally profitable.

Beau didn't know why she was with us but said it likely that she had had a tiff with her boy friend, a big publisher whose name was something like William Bamdolf First, and wanted to make him jealous.

We put Mary in the Chinese room and the housekeeper gave her the very nicest nightie in her hope chest. Beautiful Mary hung around a couple of days and apparently had no intention of departing so we arranged a little cruise on one of the yachts, named from a drug supposed by the ancient Greeks to have the power of causing forgetfulness of sorrow, and on this cruise went Mary.†

She probably thought Beau was going too, but he was very busy and couldn't get away.

The Captain had been instructed to delay return for several days but they came back soon and Mary left, still sans baggage and sans jewels, and our housekeeper burned up the once lovely nightie cherished for so long in its treasure box.

---

* "Mary Davis" is Marion Davies (1897-1961), the Ziegfeld girl, actress, and screenwriter who was the mistress of millionaire newspaper tycoon William Randolph Hearst (1863-1951).
† Davies stayed in the Cathay Bedroom, described in one account as "a showcase of chinoiserie." Davies took a cruise on Deering's yacht, *Nepenthe*.

A short time later a beautiful present arrived from New York, for Beau from Mary, so to be gallant - though truly disgusted - he asked me to wire Tiffanys to forward appropriate gift to her without delay.

We never had the pleasure of seeing Mary in person again, but I guess she is all right because I see her in the movies now and then, and unless the jewels she wears are paste she has plenty of diamonds now.

* *

Beau knew there should be a life size portrait of himself for posterity - oh no, not his; but yes, someone's.

At this time John Sargent, the great portrait painter, was in America on a pleasure jaunt, and he came down to make us a visit.

Beau was delighted when the eminent one expressed the wish to do a likeness of his classic profile, and for a setting Sargent chose the patio with its airy luxury - an inspiring picture of massive columns, stone balconies, tropic plants and Spanish tile flooring.

The easel was placed close to the gorgeous macaws, those glorious birds who perched day after day, uncaged, on standards of gold, and challenged the beauty of all man-made creations in this earthly Paradise.

For a long time Sargent worked on this portrait and it was intended to be cherished through the generations. When completed it was to be placed on the secret door of the guest room (Nans) adjoining Beau's Louis XVth.*

* The secret door connects the Espagnolette Bedroom to Deering's bedroom via the balcony.

On entering one morning I saw the completed canvas in our office salon.

> Beau said "Well, how do you like it?"
> After quite some reflection and hesitation as to expressing just what was on my mind, I replied:
> "I don't like it - you look too stern".
> Beau shrugged his shoulders, grinned and said:
> "Huh, it's no good, guess I'll give it to my brother to place among his Zorns, Whistlers, Childe Hassams and others. Sargent painted brother, too, and he don't like his so we'll make a fair exchange and be satisfied".

I never saw either portrait again.

* *

(Sketch four)*

Our next distinguished luncheon guest was another great actress, Madame Detrova.†

I guess she would be very interesting if you could see her face to face, but all during her visit she talked through a heavy veil. Beau said she had skin trouble, I don't know.

---

* Paist depicts John Singer Sargent composing his portrait of James Deering in Vizcaya's East Loggia. The setting may be discerned by the awnings over the arched doors and the model of a caravel suspended from the center of the ceiling.
† "Madame Detrova" is Olga Petrova, who appeared in "The Life Mask," directed by Billie Burke, at Vizcaya in 1918.

THE PORTRAIT

SKETCH 4

We had luncheon in the breakfast room, and the great lady did then manage to lift the transparent face covering now and then in order to partake of bits of quail, an olive, and to sip Sparkling Burgundy.

(SKETCH FIVE)*

This breakfast room was a small cozy place with a lovely marble, nude lady, fountain in the corner.

You see, Beau had a sense of humor, and when entertaining the ladies he would have the fountain turned on, so that the constant dripping of water would remind his guests of other things.

Anyway, disgusted Detrova, left the table three times and Beau felt the luncheon was a huge success.

****

My illusions of the heavenly beauty of movie actresses were shattered forever when Connie Tolmege appeared on the scene and requested the privilege of making a few close-ups on the property.†

For years she had been my screen ideal and I had worshiped her as a Goddess; never a picture but that I was first on the scene to again idolize at her shrine.

Beau had granted permission for her Company to take pic-

---

* Deering and his guest are shown in a setting that does not exactly equate with any of Vizcaya's spaces. There is a figural fountain in the formal Dining Room. However, the furnishings and broad windows are more suggestive of the second-floor Breakfast Room.

† "Tolmege" is Constance Talmadge (1898-1973), the silent film star best known for D. W. Griffith's *Intolerance* (1916). Talmadge filmed outdoor scenes for her 1921 film *Lessons in Love* at Vizcaya, along with fellow actors Kenneth Harlan ("Marlin") and Flora Finch, whom Altemus mentions below.

THE FOUNTAIN

SKETCH 5

tures on the terraces and in the gardens, but by no means in the house.

It was with a great deal of trepidation I strolled down the lovely cascaded path toward the main entrance to the villa to meet my dream girl, and here is what shattered the dream I knew.

Men were at work arranging cameras and placing tables and chairs. As I drew nearer there was an old weather beaten Ford in the driveway circle.

In the rear seat of this touring car reclined a girl and a boy - so it appeared - both with feet on top of the front seat and heads on the top of the back seat.

Both were smoking and appeared half dead. The girl, Connie, was very thin and her coarse straw colored hair and unsightly skin were not pleasant to look upon. The youth, Kenneth Marlin, was a fadeout also, at least so far as I was concerned.

How the screen can flatter - its no wonder screen stars make so few personal appearances.

Connie asked if I would care to sip tea at one of the tables and be atmosphere in the picture. Of course I was thrilled to death and months later, when the picture was released, I sat through the film three times to get a flash of my white tam-o-shanter.*

In the Company was Flora Finch, the tall, angular comedian we all used to enjoy and love so much. She had her daughter with her and she was a dear. Why doesn't Flora make a comeback as Marie Dressler has done; she's equally funny and surely another John Bunny could be found and such a duo would cer-

---

* The final scene of Lessons in Love (see photograph on p. ix) was filmed on Vizcaya's South Terrace. It shows Constance Talmadge on a bench in the foreground and three women sitting around a circular table in the background. The woman at the center of the circular table is wearing a white tam-o'-shanter, apparently confirming Altemus's account.

tainly put Marie and Polly, Laurel and Hardy, and all the other funnies to greater effort.

Of all the celebreties of stage and screen, to whom it was my privilege to show the treasures in this mansion of Beau's, Flora Finch was the only one who sensed appreciation of the beautiful without asking its price.

✶✶✶✶✶✶✶✶✶✶✶✶✶✶✶✶✶✶✶✶✶✶✶✶✶✶✶✶✶✶

Beau lived in this villa six months of each year - December through May - then to Gold Coast in June; Rue de la Paix, July to October; Fifth Avenue in November.*

After the holidays were over and we were not quite so busy he would usually begin to think about his annual party; to attend one of which was an event of a lifetime.

Now to be invited to one of these gala events it was essential to be a WHO - a relative, friend, mistress, gigolo, daughter or son of a WHO.

These parties usually lasted a week or two, and fifty house guests, with almost as many visiting maid and valets, took up all available space.†

A party would start on Wednesday, when private cars would arrive from all points north and then be sidetracked on Beau's tracks for about ten days. Some nearby guests would arrive by auto, or plane, but mostly they came by rail or yacht.

On Thursday or Friday everyone would feel at home - by Saturday or Sunday they had forgotten they had a home - and

---

* Deering maintained homes in Chicago, on Lake Shore Drive; in Neuilly-Sur-Seine, on the outskirts of Paris; and on Fifth Avenue in New York.

† Altemus appears to have overstated Vizcaya's size as the house does not have enough bedrooms to accommodate fifty guests and their staff.

the next Wednesday or Thursday they were coming back into their right minds and began to think about going home.

Beau was a splendid host; he believed that a weeks gayety should permit everyone to completely forget all trouble and care and that the proper way to start such a frame of mind was to become conveniently tight.

Although prohibition was the evil then, as it is still, Beau had had the foresight to take care of this problem. When the estate was designed, previous to the Volstead act, he knew it wouldn't be long before America would be as dry as Carrie Nation, so he had a casino - about the size of an average home - built on the property.*

This elaborate casino was high up on a mound, but the artificial mound had secret chambers below, and in this underground hideaway was a five hundred thousand dollar shipment of rare brandies, wines, liquors and cordials, all labeled and stored away in rows upon rows - enough firewater to last Beau and his guests for the remainder of their lives.†

All these beautiful bottles came to Eden at one time; a boat chartered in New York meeting the consignment from France, and then the entire lot sailing south for its secret resting place.

Before the guests had arrived at least a weeks supply of beverages had been transferred from the Casino to the guest rooms and as Beau's friends and acquaintenances were not good at resisting anything the varied colored cocktail glasses on the silver salvers were not turned upside down.

---

* Indeed, Deering had an extensive supply of fine liquor brought to Vizcaya prior to the passage of the Volstead Act of 1920 banning the production, sale, and transport of "intoxicating liquors."
† The Casino, in the gardens designed by Colombian landscape architect Diego Suarez (1888-1974), is an elegant stucco and limestone structure with a central loggia flanked by two small rooms; it served as a garden folly and tea house. Liquor was stored beneath the Casino.

If a guest had his wife with him in one part of the mansion, and his girl friend in another, the chances of the two ladies contacting were slim, as the only time all fifty guests were in one place at the same time was the formal dinner at nine - by which hour both ladies in question would be in splendid spirits and not worried over affairs ala coeur.

These late dinners were served in the formal dining room on floor one. The service was solid gold and a practical thought that was - had glass been the mode it would have been a continual replacement expense.

During the dinner a special orchestra would render concert music from the magnificent stone boat just outside the patio.

The guests would sometimes wear the corsages of orchids and boutonnieres of gardenia, sent to their rooms daily from Beau's greenhouses, but usually only a few of the older ladies and gentlemen so adorned themselves.

The French and Italian chefs spared neither time nor expense to give these WHO WHOSES the choicest morsels the world has to offer.

When dinner was over the movie started.

All the latest foreign and American films were received each morning, news reels, comedies, songs and the same big features showing in the latest movie palaces.*

Of course it was more elevating to watch the cinema at Beau's than at a theatre - the great organ installed by Welte Mignon added to the interpretation of the feature through the clever fingers of New York's one and only organist, who came down for the party - and with tables and chairs cosily arranged before

* Deering screened films from the Pathescope Company in Vizcaya's Courtyard.

the screen, the guests could not only see the picture, hear the accompanying melodies, imbibe freely in continuous highballs and even fall asleep - if so inclined - without someone in back pricking them with a hat pin or an ugly usher rushing 'em to the lobby.

During the sob stuff the great organ would cease, and lovely strains of "Heart bowed down" or "Hearts and Flowers" would peal forth from the gold piano and ancient harp in the music room. Artists playing these instruments were engaged specially for the party and a good time was had by all.

After the movie the Penelopes usually turned in as the clocks would be hitting on solo. Husbands would lag behind with Beau for final night-caps.

Girl friends, who had been resting since eleven P.M. would reappear and now was the proper time for merrymaking in the swimming pool down through the billiard room.

Sweet daddies and their baby dolls now started the big fun of the day.

There were no Ederles or Weismullers in these swimming contests, but the feats of skill and courage displayed by these big bosses and their it-girls were record breakers.

This swimming pool is probably the only one of its kind in the world. From the Billiard room and down a winding stairway the guests would enter a subterranean passageway sufficiently dim to be interesting with its sea shell bulbs of ivory and coral. A few moments stroll through a grotto of rock crystal and then a fairyland vision of a pool generous in proportion and lavish with marble and adornment.*

---

* Vizcaya's pool is partially covered by the grotto, with the ceiling designed by artist Robert Winthrop Chanler, described above. The pool is next to the house, not in the gardens.

This pool was a secluded spot in the heart of a formal Italian garden - far from the house and prying eyes.

Surrounding the pool were hundreds of Australian pines with their dense foliage completely shielding any bathing party from the world outside.

Only the tropic moon could ever know what the philanderers and their filomels found so satisfying in this pool and even romantic moonlight couldn't penetrate the awning roofed cabanas in the pines.

Besides the seashell entrance the pool had two other underground exits - one leading to the casino with its sawdust bar supervised by an old cocktail server from Bathhouse Johns - and one to a Turkish bath the stupendiousness and grandeur of which probably makes Nero shake a wicked hip in his crypt.

After a plunge in water tempered to pleasantry and then an hour's orgie in the bar sipping everything from sloe gin to absinthe and listening to modernistic nocturnes by the Hawaiian octoroons, these playtime boys and their less serious girl friends would visit the Turkish bath for a final rub-down before calling it a night. It was a dreamy group that eventually wandered back through the grotto, billiard room, and up to its respective quarters to slumber until noon the following day.

Party weeks were not such busy ones for me as Beau didn't happen to waken at his usual time, needed more calomel and seltzer, and was not on the job promptly at ten.

My assistant and I usually spent these festival times in checking up reports coming from boats, greenhouses, vegetable gardens, the dairy, grocery and market bonuses paid to chefs, Yacht Captains, etc. etc. A party at this mansion rarely cost under a hundred thousand dollars, the detail account of which kept us pleasantly occupied until the guests had left for home.

Among those at these house-warmings were many of the serious type, and for these Beau also planned weeks in advance for their amusement.

America's foremost tennis and golf professionals were engaged for those enjoying these sports, and for air-minded boys and girls Glenn Curtis and his latest plane were standing by, also engaged for two weeks. For the love of fishing and cruising groups three yachts and two cruisers were at their disposal.*

I am sure that if the guests of these gala events reminisce now over the extravagance of Beau's frolics it is with a sense of disgust of the wanton display of money and foolhardiness of the American people during the past decade.

* *

When the last guest had made his abstemious departure, the house had settled once more into regular routine, and my reports of this latest festivity were before him, Beau would become very serious minded.

He would criticise the extravagance of all his colleagues; the tremendous upkeep of his Neuilly palace, the Gold Coast home, the Ritz apartment and most of all our seven million dollar Eden.

In every way we would have to economize; he said it was foolish to permanently employ three men in the Chicago vaults just to clip his coupons as he was sure two could do the work;

He couldn't see why two hundred employees were necessary at Eden - surely fifty percent could be eliminated;

* Glenn Curtiss (1897-1930) was a pioneer aviator.

He didn't see why I needed a Packard and chauffeur to run around in when there were plenty of Fords on the place;*

He couldn't for the life of him understand why I put four cents on a letter when a two cent stamp would do - he said he had the valet buy a weighing machine for $2.00 and assured himself that he was right;

Why, said he, should my nephew go all through the house picking up my cigarettes, or my neice refuse to pay the vegetable bills (I had sent her) - especially when they both had millions of their own.

Beau, following one of these parties, worried himself sick over maintenance expense.

He was doing all he could to economize (to hear him tell it) hadn't he incorporated in Delaware thus cutting out much corporation expense, and wasn't he becoming a resident of Florida to eliminate inheritance tax?

For about two months we would make every sacrifice to save on this and that.

We had been in the habit of sending lots of radishes to William Jennings Bryan and roses and orchids to the new bride - the wed-in-quantity Peggy who was now Mrs. Joyce. They were neighbors, but now the great orator received fewer radishes, and the radiant Peggy only violets and sweet peas.†

****

* Deering had numerous cars, including three Packards, a Dodge, several Fords, and a Fiat.
† William Jennings Bryan (1860-1925), the populist orator, three-time presidential candidate, and secretary of state, was one of Deering's neighbors, as was Peggy Hopkins Joyce, actress and wife of millionaire railway and lumber executive James Stanley Joyce, of the Chicago-based Tremont & Gulf Railway Company and the Tremont Lumber Company.

About this time Beau's mother was ill and he felt she could not regain her health so we had to find a suitable casket in case she were to pass away.

As prompt as he was, he also believed in preparedness, so we ordered a casket to be made in bronze and when completed to be delivered to Eden and placed in his private car. In due time this beautiful ten thousand dollar burial case arrived but unfortunately we had no use for same at the moment.

It was almost a year before this bronze box came out of its hiding place and fulfilled the mission for which it was intended.

* *

After this great sorrow Beau decided to go in for serious study of the French language. Of course he was a fluent conversationalist in Spanish, French and Italian, but said he needed coaching, and inasmuch as America was still unsettled and as prohibition had ruined our country anyway, he anticipated spending more time in Paris and must delve into everything of French origin.

About a month later a new member from France came to join our household at Paradise. He was supposed to be a French Professor of the highest type but I always thought he was a German spy.

This old boy became Beau's shadow day and night and English was all but forgotten. Inasmuch as my smattering of French had become rusty, and partially to get rid of his shadow, Beau suggested that I devote an hour each morning to the serious study of the French language with the Professor.

During those lessons that old Frenchman, or German, could ask me more questions about America in English than I could define verbs in French, but as I had been suspicious of him since his arrival, I was too dumb to know anything about such un-interesting things as foreign relations, Leagues of Nations, etc.

Beau became very generous with the Professor's time. In order to get the old fellow out of sight as much as possible Beau suggested that he give half-hour lessons to many of Beau's friends, at his expense of course.

Just before Christmas Professor began to talk about pre-sents - said he expected splendid gifts from all his American friends and pupils.

It worried me to as a suitable gift, in appreciation of the hours we had spent together, and thought I was quite extrava-gant when I purchased a set of cuff buttons for $12.00.

My French lessons didn't proceed so well after that. The old fellow lost interest in either my ability to learn or in my Scotch frugalness, because he informed me that his other pupils, Mrs. Ruth Bryan Owen and others, had made him very costly presents at the Yule Tide and he didn't like plain cuff buttons anyway.*

* *

Three more years went by pleasantly at Eden and then Beau's health began to break.

He needed a secretary who could be constantly with him. He was in perpetual fear of being kidnapped and had a horror of bodyguards. His loyal valet had to rest some of the time and Beau was nervous when alone. And too, a young man secretary would probably better fit into this work, there were so many de-tails not quite the duties of the feminine.

Beau felt that America was no longer a land of personal free-

* Ruth Bryan Owen (1885-1954) was the daughter of William Jennings Bryan.

dom, he much preferred France. For sometime he had been talking of leaving Eden, with its capable management, and spending his last days at Neuilly.

Truly Beau was an unhappy, lonely soul; visualize if you can the following scene:

```
Time    -  6 P.M.
Place   -  Office - A magnificent Louis XIV
                    Salon in the home of
                    America's thirteenth richest
                    inhabitant.
Characters - Beau and his secretary

(Beau at his desk waiting to sign the days mail)
(Secretary enters - in a hurry as usual)

        - - - - - - - - - - - - - -

Beau    -  "Well, you are a little late tonight."

Secy.   -  "Yes, we had to get the reports off
            today for the auditors in Chicago and
            I didn't type your letters until the
            statements were on their way."

(Beau presses button - Valet enters)

Beau    -  "Tell Joseph to bring the Rolls to main
            entrance immediately. Miss _____ is in
            a hurry to get home."

(Beau continues to sign his mail)
(Secretary constantly glancing at wrist watch)

Beau    -  "You seem nervous - anything wrong?"
```

Secy.   –   "Why, no; no trouble at all – just
anxious to get home, I guess."

Beau   –   "Well, fancy that. Here we are in the
finest house in America and you want to
go home. I don't blame you, though, this
is a lonely place. What's so interesting
at your cottage?"

Secy.   –   "Oh, you couldn't understand. I can
hardly wait each day until my work is
over at Eden so I can hurry home.
You see, Tidbits is waiting for me.
Right now his chubby little fingers
and that cute little nose are pressed
tightly against the window pane
watching each passing car, for its time
for mummy to come home.
I don't like to disappoint him for he
tires watching when he has to wait too
long."

(Beau has put down his pen, lights a cigarette,
and takes a long sip of brandy)

Beau   –   "Well, I guess I've missed a lot in
life – you're terribly happy, aren't
you?"

Secy.   –   "Of course I am. I look forward during
my working hours to the fun of seeing
Tidbits every night, to feed him, to

build block houses and then knock them
down, to give him his bath and then
tuck him in for the night. We have our
cozy little nest all our own, plenty to
eat and all we need, we have health and
I have my work - what more could I ask
for."

Beau   -   Isn't life queer - here I am wretchedly
alone - must eat my dinner alone -
spend my evening alone - can't go into
town and walk around looking in the shop
windows, as I have so often wished to
do, because someone will spot me out
and stare as though I'm a freak in a
sideshow - can't do anything for always
eyes are watching. I wish I could trade
places with you for a day."

Secy.   -   "I'm so sorry for you - don't you see -
it's simply too much money. I tell
you whats let do. You hurry and finish
signing those letters, tell the valet
you are not eating tonight, come and
have dinner with Tidbits and me - we'd
love to have you.
Come on - why not - of course you won't
have terrapin or squab, but I bet Mammy
has some real Boston Baked Beans and
rich brown bread - Please do, just be a
poor boy for an hour."

(Beau smiled, shifted in his chair, glanced at
the button as though he were going to call his
Valet; then he looked at me and sadly said)

> "Thanks, so much. Its terribly nice
> of you to ask me, but can't you see
> that I cannot even do that. I cannot
> leave this room without at least three
> servants knowing it; to go out the main
> entrance without the butler's knowledge
> is impossible; to leave the grounds
> without the eyes of the watchmen at
> the gates noticing is inconceivable; to
> drive to your place for an hour while
> Joseph waits in the car outside means
> that before I return here at least two
> hundred people will know where I've
> been, how long I stayed, just what I did
> and just what I didn't do.
> No, I'm cursed with wealth and must
> suffer the consequences."

Secy.   -   "Yes, you're right, it wouldn't do. I'm
            sorry."

(Beau signed the few remaining letters, sealing
the last two himself before passing them over
to me.)

Secy.   -   "Goodnight, see you tomorrow."

Beau   -   "Good-night and thank you."

- - - - - - - - - -

The year was now 1921.

We had engaged a very competent fellow, a chap who had lived most of his life in France, to take over my duties as secretary; and Tidbits and I were planning a vacation someplace far away.*

Living amidst so much wealth had ceased to be of interest, so with the following letter from Beau

> "To WHOM it may concern:
>   The bearer, Miss _____
> is the best business woman I
> have ever known.
>
> _____
>
>   Ex-President of
>   Teaser and Reaper, Inc."

tucked in our grip, Tidbits and I closed our little green and white cottage in the south, said goodbye to old colored Mammy, bought a ticket and a half for The Dixie Flyer and wound our way northward to The Windy City.

* *

---

* The new secretary, Mr. Essay, was hired in 1919, with the goal of him traveling with Deering to France. Deering's health worsened while living in Paris. In September of 1925, he slipped into a coma and was placed onboard the steamship SS *Paris* to return to New York for treatment. He died en route. Altemus left Miami for Chicago in 1921 or 1922.

CHICAGO

Once a secretary, always a secretary.

The nest egg we had saved during our years in the south wouldn't last forever and Tidbits and I had been playing around for two months.

We had given the once over to every toy in Field's playroom - we could tell you about every animal in the Lincoln Park Zoo - we knew every kid at Clarendon Beach - we had sported joy rides on the top of every bus line approaching the Loop - we had even been out in the country and helped milk the cows and bring in the eggs - but time was fleeting and the check book wasn't showing any increase in deposits - therefore it was time to again search opportunity.*

It so happened that Tidbits would soon be ready for school enlightenment. He had successfully weathered the measles, the poxes, whooping-cough and all baby temperatures which cause employed mothers so many sleepless nights, and now it would take quite a nip out of our bankroll for that tonsil and adenoid

---

* Marshall Field's Department Store in the Chicago Loop—the central business district encircled by the elevated train—had a noted toy department and also delighted children with its annual animated Christmas window displays.

detachment the doctors told me was so necessary before the 'writin and rithmetic' began.

I was told that the Windy City was a splendid place in which to have anything removed and I knew that St. Joseph's Hospital on the northside was a grand place in which to be sick. Tidbits came into being there one night when I was seventeen and I hadn't forgotten those sweet and kindly Sisters who throughout the night held my hands, told me not to be afraid, placed ice-bags to my temples and gave me whiffs of ether when I begged and pleaded with them. They would be just as nice to my little one, so thither we went and Tidbits began his second fortnight in this pleasant place.*

* *

With Beau's letter in my pocket, and plenty of advice from girls I had met at the beach as to the proper procedure to secure secretarial positions in Chicago, I visited the agencies seeking my second piece of work.

These active powers, after taking all the money I had with me for so-called registration fees and exacting a promise to pay them fifty percent of my first months pay, told me of a splendid opening for just my type. However I must put the Mrs. in the archives of my memory and become a Miss again; I must be a college graduate; and as for even suggesting a Tidbits well - of course - that was simply out of the question.

I didn't like that idea of being a Miss again; neither did I approve of keeping Tidbits in the background; but still if Chicago men didn't like married women or mothers around their

---

* Altemus was in fact twenty-seven when Robert was born.

offices that was their business and I would keep my private life to myself.

It was at this stage of the game that I became a great prevaricator. The agency sent me to interview

TOWN & MALWOOD

Patent Lawyers

I told these estimable gentlemen that I was a maiden and living with my parents; that I was a graduate of Vassar and post-graduate of Smith; that my reputation was beyond reproach and gave them Beau's letter to show that I knew something about business.

The job was mine and at a splendid salary.

I wanted an apartment now that I was so nicely placed in business; Tidbits would need careful attention when released from the hospital; it would be necessary for a combination nurse-maid-housekeeper at least during the day to look after him and this all loomed up in a perfectly splendid way but it would be expensive.

Into the Personal Column of the Chicago Tribune went the following advertisement:

"Young, successful business woman with five year old son would share expenses of select apartment and maid with congenial business woman having youngster of same age."

(SKETCH FIVE-A)

This little ad. paid many a bonus in friendship and happiness. Nita answered and we found a charming apartment on Sheridan Road and moved in.

(SKETCH SIX)

Nita had a little girl, Blossom, and what a little flower she was, a lovely creature of five or six.

We located an efficient housekeeper, who would be glad to take care of the kiddies, and within a week Tidbits was home and our foresome was complete.

Nita was probably a Jewess although she claimed French as her ancestry. To describe her would be to apologize to Diana.

Her hair was raven black and she wore it parted in the middle and drawn tightly down to the nape of her neck. Her eyes were large and dark and fringed with lashes of blackest night. Her only adornment was an antique pair of jet ear-rings, which she always wore. Nita's skin was clear and alabaster white; she never used rouge probably because the full red lips of her sensuous mouth were naturally true vermillion. Though she was tall and rather voluptuous of figure I do not think she was over twenty-five.

Nita was conversant about everything except her business. No one seemed to know just what she did or where she went. She left home each morning about eight o'clock and returned for dinner at six. She had no office and to locate her in the daytime was looking for the old needle in the haystack.

We grew terribly fond of one another and I couldn't understand why she had to remain the world's zenith of mystery with me as to her working hours. She would phone my office often but when I had a message for her it would have to wait until evening.

NITA

BLOSSOM

SKETCHES 5-A AND 6

She had told me other secrets - she had not a living relative and Blossom had "growed" just like Topsy.

"Lilies of the field, neither do they toil nor spin" - but Nita was no Lily.

She cared nothing for the sheiks of the day and her evenings were for her baby and an early to bed regime. She would say she was tired and anticipated a hard days work on the morrow.

I ceased to worry about how and where she earned her money; nevertheless the dollars floated into our little haven of rest, and how.

She surprised me on my birthday with a piano; then bought herself oriental rugs, Chinese cloisienes and Satsuma; ivory cabinet pieces and other luxuries began to fill our apartment, and when I would give her an eery look she would only say

```
"I made a killing in the market today."
        or
"Believe it or not, sweetness, I played the
ponies and the gravy is rich tonight."
```

Nita liked rare wines with her dinner and through some source they arrived. Sometimes at night, when the kiddies were in the Arms of Morpheus, she would imbibe a little more than usual, but even with the most carefully put inquiries never did I hit first base as an answer to wherefrom came the where-withall.

****

Six months passed pleasantly by; everything was going smoothly both at home and at the office.

Mr. Malwood informed me that I was to have a raise in salary, that my work as his secretary had been more than satisfactory. Both he and Mr. Town - the senior partner - felt that I was a valuable addition to their firm.

Miss Hewitt, secretary to Mr. Town, had helped me a great deal in my first weeks at the office and we had become friends. She usually lunched with Mr. Town but occasionally she would take me to lunch at a speakeasy near the College Inn. She liked the place, said it was cosmopolitan, that she and Mr. Town had been lunching there for two years.*

For our lunch Miss Hewitt would order two club sandwiches and a couple of Horses Necks - the latter were pretty and expensive and unless people ordered such things they were considered hicks. One day she ordered four Horses Necks and became quite confidential.†

She told me that Town was a real guy, that outside of the office he was a true sport, that he didn't get along with his wife and for the past two years had been paying for Miss Hewitt's tuition at night law school. She said he liked the ladies but that she was his big moment.

As for Malwood, she told me he was a nut; said he was Scotch and so tight that he kept his wife worried so she would lose weight. She told me that I never would have received that raise if it hadn't been for Town, and that it wouldn't be long before

---

* The College Inn was located in the Sherman Hotel, on Randolph Street between Clark and LaSalle, as was the Panther Room, a speakeasy that featured jazz musicians, including band leader Isham Jones, and Cole Porter, Duke Ellington, and Fats Waller.

† The horse's neck was introduced as a nonalcoholic beverage but by the 1910s it was served as an alcoholic cocktail made with brandy (or bourbon) and ginger ale, with a long spiral of lemon peel draped over the edge of the glass.

she would be admitted to the bar and then she would be the junior member of that firm.

Something about those Horses Necks didn't agree with me and while she was raving on about Town and legal lore my mind was drifting out to Sheridan Road -- was he asleep -- was Blossom teasing him -- had he had his lunch -- wish I could go home.

> Miss Hewitt shook me and said "What's that -
> did you say something about going home -
> snap out of it Kiddo - drink that coffee
> straight and lets get going. Well for crying
> out loud - what are those tears for - for
> heaven's sake whats eating you?"

> "Nothing, I'm all right but I was just
> thinking of something. You know, Miss Hewitt,
> I like you and you're my friend and I'm going
> to tell you a secret - that is, if you won't
> tell."

> Miss Hewitt - "Well if its interesting, shoot,
> but make it snappy."

(SKETCH SEVEN)

I told her of Tidbits, of Nita, of Blossom; what wonderful times we had together and invited her out to dinner whenever she could make it; and all she said was

> "Why you poor kid - I'm certainly sorry for
> you - but come on now, we're late and there

TID BITS AT FIVE

SKETCH 7

```
is plenty to do on those Wilson patents this
afternoon."*
```

I wondered what she was sorry about, but glad I told her - it would be nice to know there was someone at TOWN & MAL-WOODS to whom I could talk about Tidbits.

A short time after this Mr. Town called me in his office one morning and said that Miss Hewitt had telephoned and said she was ill and would not be at the office. He asked if I would mind taking a few of his important letters before Mr. Malwood arrived.

Of course it was a pleasure to help out in any way possible and it would keep the work from piling up for Miss Hewitt.

Not only that day did I type Mr. Town's important letters but every day following. Miss Hewitt had the grippe and wouldn't be back at the office for a week at least.

About the third day in Mr. Town's private office, while dictating a brief, he stopped all of a sudden and blurted out

```
"How about having lunch with me today - I
usually talk over business affairs with Miss
Hewitt during luncheon - it saves so much
time - and there are some matters I should
like to discuss with you.
```

Something told me that Mr. Malwood wouldn't approve - that Miss Hewitt wouldn't like it - that I really shouldn't - but still he was the senior partner, wasn't he - couldn't very well refuse - wasn't he the reason for my raise - guess I'd better - so I said

```
* Most likely the Wilson patents were associated with the Thomas E.
Wilson Company, which later became Wilson Sporting Goods.
```

```
"I guess so - thanks - where will I meet
you."
```

I thought he would say the speakeasy where he and Miss Hewitt had spent so many hours together, but instead he suggested I met him at De Joghne's at one o'clock.*

Mr. Town was there when I arrived and the luncheon he ordered would have been fit for Beau's table. He suggested an appetizer but I told him I didn't need one - that I was always hungry at mealtime. I was afraid he might order a Horses Neck but he didn't, we had a respectable luncheon with just a creme de menthe after the coffee.

Nonchalantly he suggested that it might be advisable if I refrained from mentioning our luncheon at the office - thought it best not to speak of it even to Miss Hewitt when she returned.

I assured him that mum was the word and left alone, as he said he had some business to attend to at the Club before returning to the office.

```
* * * * * * * * * * * * * * * * * * * * * * *
```

```
State and Madison Streets,
         5 P.M.
```

It was a bitterly cold afternoon just before Christmas.

We had had a busy week at the office and not sufficient time for an hour's luncheon. I wanted to buy some toys for the children and the only available time was after five o'clock.

The snow was piled high in the gutters: it had been snowing

---

* De Jonghe's, a French restaurant at 12 East Monroe Street, was known as one of the best places to dine in the city.

for two days and Dick Fox's efficient white wings were doubling their forces to clear the Loop for the Christmas shoppers.*

Happy mothers and dads, loaded down with packages, boxes and Christmas trees, were wending their different ways towards any available transportation for home.

Half walking and skating on the icy sidewalk between Monroe and Madison Streets I noticed an unusual mob of shoppers gathering at the corner. My usual curiosity asserted itself and with still faster strides I wedged myself into the crowd.

An accident on State Street was an every day occurrence - 'but it was so cold tonight and just before Christmas too - ooh I hope no one is hurt'.

The siren of an ambulance was competing with the screeching of car wheels as I pushed into the center of that group.

I could see streaks of crimson in the snow and shuddered, but couldn't resist another look.

Yes, another accident - a woman - an old woman - lying on her side perfectly still. Apparently she was unconcious - a shabby shawl was pinned closely around her neck - her clothes and shoes looked shapeless and were torn - a bonnet with a heavy black veil had shifted to the side displaying a mass of grey disheveled hair. In her hand she clasped a round tray in which there appeared to be a few coins.

An officer pushed us back - he said she had been struck by a truck - one of those hit and miss drivers who do not stop.

They lifted her gently and placed her on the stretcher - a man in white placed his head to her chest and then brushed the hair from her face to look at her eyes. As he did this her bon-

* Richard T. Fox supervised the Citizens' Street Cleaning Bureau, a civic group organized to clean and sweep streets as well as remove snow.

net and what appeared to be a wig of grey hair slipped off the stretcher and into the snow.

Another glance at the stretcher - black hair - those black earrings - then I saw the face - Nita - Nita - I screamed again and again.

An officer grabbed me as they were lifting the stretcher and sliding it into the ambulance. He asked me if I knew her.

```
"Yes - Nita" I screamed again.
```

I remember the officer pushing me into an automobile and following that ambulance to a hospital.

I remember a nurse giving me something in a glass and officers questioning me.

I told them all I could - she was glorious Nita, my pal - she had no relatives but a baby who lived with me - I didn't know why she was dressed up with that wig and those old clothes - wouldn't they please take me to her.

```
They took me to the operating room and I stood
inside the door. She was moaning - "Blossom -
truck - money - Blossom - they thought I would
squeal - money - Blossom - they said they would
get me - money - Blossom - saw it coming - tried
to dodge - Blossom."
```

I begged the Officer to hurry and bring Blossom to the hospital for Nita was calling for her - they told me she didn't know what she was saying - that it wouldn't be best - that it was a case of only a little while.

They took me home and would telephone me later.

Nita passed away that night.

The nurse told me later that before Nita died there were moments of semi-conciousness in which she raved of being a stenographer in lawyers offices but always discharged when they found out she had a baby - of joining a gangster group for lots of money and becoming an old woman beggar as a blind - of the big boss daily slipping her a bill pinned to which were instructions for the gang - of one of the gang later dropping a coin into the tray and receiving the note from the higher up - of trying to quit the gang but couldn't, she knew too much - of seeing the truck coming and trying to dodge - of putting lots of money in a safety deposit box - of Blossom - Blossom.

* * * * * * * * * * * * * * * * * * *

We found quite a sum of money, jewels and a very generous insurance policy in Nita's safety deposit box. Blossom was to be paid a goodly amount, monthly, over a period of years. The policy had been taken out about a year before - probably such a tragic end had been anticipated.

Nita - my glorious Carmen - was gone - now I had two children instead of one.

* *

A week passed - I hadn't been near the office - had sent them a note saying I was ill - and had Margaret, our house-keeper, call up each day and tell Mr. Malwood I would be back in a day or so.

Of course Blossom couldn't understand and she cried nights for Nita; Margaret was kind and would tell her stories and rock her to sleep; daytimes Blossom seemed content playing with new toys, but the evenings were lonely for all of us.

Everything seemed upside down. I thought busy days back at the office would adjust matters - at least so far as I was concerned - but it didn't prove so to be.

When I returned I sensed a strangeness about Miss Hewitt - she was neither cordial or friendly - and I couldn't see that she and Mr. Town were even on speaking terms. He kept calling me in to take his dictation and Mr. Malwood's work was not getting the time it should.

Finally one day Mr. Malwood called for me - he said he was sorry that I had deceived him - that he had ascertained from Miss Hewitt that I had been lunching with Mr. Town, that I was a married woman and that I had a child, and he thought it best for all concerned that he secure another secretary.

I don't remember saying anything to anyone - I did take my few personal articles from my desk and went home and cried it all out on Margaret's lap.

* *

January passed, February was passing and it was still snowing - the coldest winter I ever knew - but the apartment was cozy and warm and I was glad to escape those cold morning rides to the Loop.

During the long hours indoors Margaret told me about everyone in the apartment house - she knew every man's business and all about their wives and sweethearts - she knew just which apartments sported bootleggers - she knew who paid their bills - all about that couple directly over us, they were not married, - she knew secrets about that auburn haired lady on the first floor who had so many people driving up in taxicabs at all hours of the day and night.

> "Margaret, how in the world did you find out
> all these things", I asked her;

and she told me that Susan, maid to the lady across the hall, knew Anna maid to the lady on the ground floor, that Anna's sister Lulu worked for the couple upstairs; that Susan, Anna, Lulu and she visited back and forth when they were not busy.

Margaret told me that the lady across the hall felt so sorry for me and wanted to drop in some morning, that she was busy afternoons and evenings playing poker but hoped that she could say hello some morning about eleven.

I didn't imagine I would be of interest to any poker-playing ladies, inasmuch as I knew nothing about the game, but the apartment was lonely and I told Margaret it would be nice to meet Susan's mistress.

It wasn't an unexpected tap on my door the next morning at eleven; I was ready and waiting for my visitor.

And, what a whirlwind blew in.

She was young, not yet twenty, rather plump and very pretty; as blonde as Nita had been dark.

Susan had told her all about our trial and how I had lost my position - she was so sorry and wanted to be a friend and help out in any way she could - she said it was all wrong for one to stay in the house and mope, that she played poker every after- noon and some evenings, and if I had a hundred dollars she would introduce me to her friends.

Margaret made us some coffee and I became fascinated with the Southern drawl of this stranger. She said the only slow thing about her was her speech, that she was a daughter of the old south, from 'Atlanter' she said, and her name was Babs.

(SKETCH SEVEN-A)

Babs said she believed in progress, that when she was sweet sixteen she went to a band concert and heard Creatori's band; she fell in love with the looks of Creatori's son and from that time on she had no use for Atlanter, Home or Mother.

Babs told me she was a chip off the old block because Pater had left home sometime before and went to Chicago to make Mickelberry's sausage; she heard that the Band was in Chicago and it didn't take her anytime at all to put a tooth brush, nightie and other goods into the old kit bag, scrape up the fare to the big city, say goodbye to Mater and travel northwest.

She met a nice looking chap on the train, also enroute to the Windy City. He was a ladies tailor and as she would need pretty tailor made clothes in which to be progressive and as the young man was unattached, she proposed marriage and was accepted. They left the train at Hammond, Indiana; tied the knot; and, set up housekeeping across the hall from our apartment two years before.

Babs said she wasn't successful with the Creatori search but Chicago had so many interesting features that she didn't waste time grieving over anything.

She told me she had only been in the Windy City a few weeks before she was making money - she had a luncheon racket - she would call up big business men and make luncheon dates at a certain Roof - the more she ate and drank the more she made; said she was fond of champagne and delicacies - and when the bill was paid she was credited with ten percent. Usually, she said,

BABS

at sixteen

SKETCH 7-A

it was advisable to lunch with married men because they liked to dine in private booths and that was more expensive than just eating. Her husband was rather dumb, she said; he always had a sandwich in his tailor shop, so she had her lunches at the Roof, the Annex, the Arena or other points south every day and did well.

I asked Babs if she wouldn't have another cup of coffee but she declined - said she had had stomach trouble for the past few months and her physician, Dr. Lerner of the Ravenswood Hospital, placed her on a strict diet with two cups of coffee daily only, and no other stimulants. Said she no longer went to downtown lunches but was making money now playing poker and hoped I could join her some day soon.

Assuring her I would be delighted to go, if she would teach me to play, she said it was time to hurry on and kissed me goodbye.

What a beautiful world - still snowing and so much happiness if only one looked for it.

Blossom and Tidbits ceased putting finishing touches to a snow-man to throw a snow ball at Babs as she ran from the steps to a waiting car at the curb. She waved and smiled but don't think she approved of snow-flakes spotting that jaunty chappeau and chic newly tailored suit.

```
'Babs was smart all right - no one should
sit around and mope - it would be nice to
go to a poker party but why the hundred
dollars - wouldn't spend that much to meet
even the Prince of Wales - only a few hundred
left in the bank - must get busy on another
job - yes, tomorrow better visit the agency
```

again but no more lawyers - they don't like
children much.'

That evening at dinner I was telling Margaret and the kiddies all about looking for another position in the morning, when in blew Babs again, this time through the kitchen, and said she was going to take me to a poker party in about an hour.

I told her I didn't have a hundred dollars and if I had wouldn't dare spend it. She told me not to be silly, that she was going to take me just to look on, that it wouldn't cost me a cent, and after the game they always had a buffet supper and we would have a good time.

Babs said her husband would drive us to the party but for me not to mention anything about a hundred dollars, said he knew she played cards but thought they were ladies social games and he was glad she had these card clubs as it kept her occupied while he was working.

Confidentially, Babs told me that the players, with the exception of herself, were all rich women, but they never allowed their husbands to play because it didn't work out - that only wealthy bachelors, widowers and other women's husbands played poker with them. Dr. Lerner had lots of money and he loaned her funds when she lost.

Bab's husband drove us to the party and said if needed to phone him at his shop.

A maid asked us in and took our wraps.

It was a spacious and beautifully furnished apartment, but you could have heard a pin drop it was so quiet.

The maid disappeared and Babs whispered to make myself at home, that we were a little late and for me to keep absolutely quiet until the game was over.

As she left me I watched her tip-toe through the vestibule into an immense dining room ablaze with light. The scintillating room was a mass of crystal, lavish with cut-glass sparkling on buffets, sideboards and cabinets; mirrors everywhere; and chandeliers with hundreds of prisms diffusing colored rays in all directions.

In the center of the room men and women were sitting around a circular table, and if Capone could have seen the jewels on those ladies he wouldn't have needed a beer racket.*

No one spoke to Babs as she took a place at the table beside a distinguished looking gentleman in a tuxedo; he smiled and gave Babs a knowing glance as he touched her hand; I wondered if he were Dr. Lerner.

Excepting the click of cards and chips, the swinging of a door through which two agile colored maids kept passing through, and the gurgling of cocktails from shakers to long stemmed glasses, I couldn't hear a sound. It was all so still and awe inspiring I dared not move. And, when the telephone on a desk beside me screeched forth its rasping call I was literally scared to death.

A maid rushed in and grabbed the receiver and said "Hello". I could hear a man's excited voice and the maid's soft reply

```
"No, she's not here - no one here - Madam is
not at home - I'm all alone - sorry."
```

Another screech from that telephone but this time the maid simply lifted off the receiver and told me to leave it off.

---

* Altemus refers, of course, to Alphonse "Al" Capone, who grew to fame as a result of the "beer wars" during Prohibition, in which rival gangs sought to control the underground liquor market as well as gambling and prostitution.

This was the strangest home I had ever been in. No one but that maid had spoken to me - no one had spoken to any one - there was a buzzing in that receiver and then that, too, became discouraged and was quiet.

I could see Babs smiling at the gentleman on her left as they kept passing her stacks of chips. She must be making lots of money I thought.

My eyes were heavy and thought of my plans for tomorrow - if I could sneak in there and get my wraps it would be nice to wade home through the snow in the moonlight. Bab's wouldn't miss me and it wasn't far to go - wonder who is making that noise in the lobby outside - better ask them to please be quiet.

Slowly and quietly I slipped to the entry door and turned the knob but before the door was opened an inch someone pushed that door and me into the wall. Something wild and muttering rushed in and through to that brilliantly illuminated room; I could see him tilt back a chair, grab the lovely blonde by the neck and drag her into the vestibule where I was standing too frightened to move.

```
He kept raving
"Not here huh - well I'll show you and
your friends whether you're here or not."
She was crying "Oh Ernie please don't. Oh
please."
```

Beside me was a tall bronze vase and I thought the proper thing to do was to let that light squarely on Ernie's dome, but at that moment the lovely blonde hit the gentleman in the face with a big gold mesh bag which kindly opened and emptied dozens of gold pieces at my feet.

The argument continued and I picked up the gold pieces safely within my reach. Everything was in an uproar, people were rushing here and there; Babs said we were going home and to get my wraps.

The battle was on for a few more minutes and then the mauler was induced to have a drink.

The lady was still sobbing when I held out the gold pieces and told her they dropped from her bag. She said she didn't want his filthy money, that she would throw them into the fireplace, that I should keep them.

Dr. Lerner took us home in his big limousine and I noticed he and Babs held hands all the way. He said he was sorry Ernie couldn't stay sober, that it was the second time he had staged such an outrage. The doctor said if Ernie would stay home once in a while his wife probably wouldn't play poker; that they owned one of Chicago's biggest department stores and with their wealth it was too bad they couldn't be happy too.*

The Doctor let us out at the corner near our apartment and on the way home Babs told me she won over a hundred dollars. Passing the newel post I gave her a look-in on four twenty dollars gold pieces in my palm.

That was my first and last poker game.

* Ernie is likely Ernest J. Lehmann Jr., owner of the Fair Department Store, commonly regarded as Chicago's first department store.

PIERRE DUVAL

Margaret called me early in the morning and after kissing the youngsters goodbye I left for the Loop and third opportunity.

The Agency told me an architect required the services of a secretary and would be most choice in his selection; he had recently arrived from Switzerland and preferred a secretary with knowledge of at least conversational French; would I care to interview the gentleman?

Architecture made me think of Beau and Eden - yes, I thought such work would be most interesting.

It was about ten in the morning when I found the address on Division Street. After climbing four flights of stairs the following placard caught my eye:

```
   _____
   :   PIERRE DUVAL   :
   :                  :
   :     Architect    :
   _____
```

I gave a gentle tap and after quite some wait the door opened and there stood he. The gentleman may have been awake but didn't look it as he rubbed his eyes and forehead with a sleeve of his blue garb - don't know whether he was dressed in pajamas or a new style smock. His hair was as disheveled as was the room into which he politely bade me enter. Excusing himself for a moment 'my take-in at a glance' observed the following:

On the right seemed to be a sort of bed or sleeping couch, beneath which were magazines, a rat trap, soiled linens, torn papers, cameras, cigarette stubs and other things best not mentioned.

To the left stood a drafting table aligned with with pencils galore, blue-prints, triangles, T-squares, a broken banjo and some rusted bronze.

On a table were photographs, letters, boxes, more cigarette stubs, feathers, snake skins and some artificial flowers in a milk bottle.

Canvasses stood in rows all around the room - pictures from Alaskan mountains to the Rue de la Paix. Over in a corner was an unfinished easel upon which was a truly beautiful September Morn. Some antiquated paper tulips, daffodils and forget-me-knots were also in this corner and on a weather beaten chest of drawers were some good vases, a music box, more cigarete stubs and, believe it or not, a nice clean unused ash tray.

The drapes next caught my eye. On the street side were nailed some old faded, unhemmed and ragged blue denim streaks of color. To the north windows were tacked white cheesecloth beautified with dabs of every hue - probably thrown on by brushes when painting or maybe these curtains were brush wipers. These unsanitary hangings were adorned by a lovely old Spanish grille outside.

Hanging from the ceiling were canvasses and etchings worth while, I thought - oils, water colors and pastels, - modernistic breastless and hipless nudes, a Venus and a swan, a portrait of the caretaker's daughter, a longshot at Ascot or maybe a hotshot of Rosa Bonheurs.*

The rugs in this office deserve some expression. There were two of the rag rug variety and due to maturity were convulsed in wrinkles; however, they did harmonize with the tout ensemble.

My word, thought I, what a terrible place and what on earth can he possibly want of a secretary, looks more like an artist's studio than the office of an architect.

Pierre had donned something that looked like a cross between a kimona and a straight jacket and very courteously came forward and asked that I be seated and state my mission. He apoligized for the disordered studio and the lateness of the hour for arising but he had been working most of the night and overslept. If I didn't mind he would breakfast now, so he swallowed a concentrated tablet, which he said was coffee, and some other pills which he explained were a combination of wheat and yeast.

```
"Now, my dear young lady, what can I do for
you," said he.
```

I told him I had been sent to him by the Agency as they informed me he needed the services of a secretary.

```
"Oh, yes, yes, how silly of me to forget,
I did instruct the charming little lady
there to find me a secretary who could speak
French. Right at the moment there is nothing
on the boards; however I expect something
to come up at anytime and its best to be
prepared, don't you think so," said he.
```

* Rosa Bonheur (1822-1899) was a famous French painter and sculptor.

I told him I thought it was.

He said we might need a typewriter a little later on but for the present he used a liquid substance that resembled ink when it dried and if I could do simple printing we could manage somehow.

Pierre said he liked me exceedingly and he was sure we could do some very good work together and give the world something really worth while. He said he anticipated designing a Swiss chalet for the daughter of an American millionaire but so far the contract had not been signed, and he preferred some retainer even before submitting sketches.

The gentleman hoped I could start right in this morning as he would like so very much to do my profile for a magazine cover he was to submit late in the afternoon.

By this time I didn't know whether I was to be engaged for a secretary, a printer, a model, or what, but there was something about the earnestness and suavity of this dignified person together with the reckless abandon of the exotic office that aroused sufficient interest to linger a while.

```
"Mr. Duval, I really would enjoy very much
working with you, but may I ask just what
remuneration you feel this position is
worth."
```

Said Pierre -

```
"Oh now, don't give a thought to the amount
of pay. It really, you know, is so decidedly
ordinary to speak of dollars, that I rarely
discuss the filthy subject. Whatever you
received at your last position, plus whatever
```

percentage of increase, due to progression,
you think fair, is perfectly satisfactory
to me. Now then take off your things and we
will get to work without further ado."

"But, Mr. Duval, you see I have two small
children and my responsibilities are many,
and,"

Mr. Duval - "Oh, now, isn't that splendid, why I
really cannot believe it - thats perfectly
marvelous and all the more reason we should
not waste words, so come along now and take
off your wraps."

Whether it was the charm of this fellow, the strange atmosphere, or my inate curiousity, at any rate I decided to give this work a try out.

Arriving mornings promptly at ten and knocking loudly enough to awaken and give Pierre a chance to let me in and get himself into his Specialist, from which he usually emerged in a semi-sleepy but respectable state of body and mind, my first job was to tidy up this nest as well as I could. The cleaning up process was annoying to Pierre, but I couldn't refrain from picking up here and there and sweeping the cigarette stubs into a corner. He seemed to enjoy having me around and the first thing I knew I was running to the delicatessen for this and that, to the camera store for films, to the drug store for Whiz Bang and cigarettes and to the speak-easy for other things.

By the way Pierre had no drinking water in the studio. There had been some trouble with the water pipes a few months before and the janitor had failed to have this matter taken care of; Handsome, as to myself I called Pierre, didn't mind; he said it would be taken care of sooner or later and in the meantime he was using peroxide for cleansing and wine and moonshine for drinking.

The first few days I managed nicely without water but Margaret had placed some salt mackerel before me at breakfast on the fourth day and I became thirsty by the time I reached the office. One sip of wine didn't quench that desire for water so I helped myself to another nip.

While posing for a head and shoulder sketch Pierre complained of my not holding the pose. It didn't please me to be criticized in this manner and as I felt nervous and sleepy thought it would be best to go home. Handsome was courteous even when piqued and suggested I call it a day. A resolution was in order to eat no more mackerel, although it seemed strange that other secretaries could handle Horses Necks and things and I couldn't manage two sips of wine.

The next day Pierre had some letters he wanted me to answer. They were mostly "Accounts Rendered, Kindly Remit" ones. He told me to tell them that he had been so rushed with work he had been unable to get to the bank to obtain a checkbook, but he would do so within the next few days, at which time payment would go forward immediately.

This was encouraging to me as at my old salary, plus the fifty percent increase I felt was justified owing to the extra housekeeping and modeling I was doing, Tidbits, Blossom and I could indulge in that suitcase radio thing we heard for the first time a few nights before.

The first five days of the week passed quickly and pleasantly as the new work appealed strongly to me but was disappointed on Saturday to find the office without its occupant. There was a note for me penned by Pierre on Friday night - he had been invited to a week end party and would see me Monday.

Bab's husband was busy at the shop on Saturday nights and as no poker game was scheduled, she dropped in to spend the evening with me. Dr. Lerner happened to be in the neighborhood and he, too, stopped in for a moment.

I told them all about my work and that it was disappointing not to receive a check for the weeks work.

Babs said Pierre probably went to the party to get a square meal, that architects and artists were delightful dinner companions when guests of their clients; and, Dr. Lerner suggested keeping my eye open for a different type of work, something more substantial in a downtown office building.

On Monday I told Pierre we would mail out the checks we wrote about if he had the new check book, but he simply would not talk money - it was distasteful and besides he never even carried money with him, no one knew whether a leper or a small poxer had it previous and it was suicidal to carry around the dirty lucre.

For two weeks this reasoning was all right but after I had housekeeped, modeled, printed, and ran errands for three weeks, during which period Handsome was always too busy to get a checkbook, I had drawn quite a sum from my savings account. Being practical and Scotch this didn't appeal as being a hot proceeding and I decided to look elsewhere for a less interesting but more profitable duty.

Now Pierre and I during our three weeks cooperation had grown quite fond of one another and I dreaded informing him that my mercenary tendencies urged that I seek another position, but there were the kiddies expenses going on and too, I was to have my wisdom tooth extracted and that bill must be paid.

We held a conference for two and a tear dropped into my cocktail before this secretaryship was over. Pierre told me he wanted a souvenier to remember me by and requested the wisdom tooth to be removed on the morrow.

I sent him the tooth by special delivery and consoled myself that his treasuring of this piece of my tissue should compensate for the sheckles still coming to me when and if he found time to get a check book.

****

SLEUTHS

The wisdom tooth was gone and I felt blue and discouraged. Pierre had been wonderful and it had been so much fun tidying up his office and taking care of things that it was with reluctant heart I answered the following advertisement in The Chicago Tribune:

"Secretary Wanted. Clever and fearless young lady, unusual and interesting work, pay commensurate with ability."

The "fearless" aroused my old inquisitiveness and an investment for a two cent stamp seemed trivial for an adventure; hence the following scrawl developed into an interview of surprises:

"Am a thoroughly experienced secretary; second to none in ingenuity, Marathonian endurance and a chiseler."

Came an answer:

"Kindly call at Penthouse,

The Glorida, Lake Shore
Drive, Monday 9 P.M."

Now any job calling for interview at 9 P.M. must not only be exceptional but good. I decided that here was an old foggy, probably lousy with gold, who had some hobby of looking through glasses at the terrace between the Boulevard and the Lake, copying George Arliss' Man who Played God, and wished to send letters to the distraut; or, maybe it was some "stew" sufficiently sobered to wish to write his memoirs.*

There is always something about Chicago's Gold Coast that makes one feel several degrees higher in importance than when strolling on Clark Street, and by the time the Glorida loomed into view I wouldn't have spoken to a Boston Lodge had I met one.

It was just nine as I entered the elevator. The luxury of this lift, the gorgeous gold braid of the lifter man, and the length of the lifting, elevated me to the millionaire class before reaching this home in the sky.

It seemed a wait of hours before the butler ushered me into the boudoir of a woman, one glance at whom made me creep; she would have been the world's nightmare to a swain in search of romance.

To describe this creature would be simply to visualize a great bulk of adipose tissue, feminine of course due to the ribbons and laces of her scanty raiment and the blonde tresses long since dead from years of peroxide.

---

* The Man Who Played God is a 1932 film that starred actor George Arliss as a celebrated pianist who becomes deaf and spends his subsequent days looking out through powerful binoculars from his New York apartment window at park goers in Central Park, reading their lips and then trying to intervene to solve their problems.

The face that looked so scrutinizingly into mine was a lifted one, for the eyes were almost Chinese, with the skin a porcelain mask which dared not smile.

The constantly twitching short and pudgy fingers kept perfectly in tune with the tapping on the rug of the right pedal extremity.

(SKETCH EIGHT)

This woman was probably fifty-five but looked older. She was extremely nervous and lighted two cigarettes at once as she sipped at a highball before speaking.

Finally she said:

> "My dear young lady I have an unusual mission
> for a clever person. A woman is preferable as
> I do not trust men.
>
> This work is in a sense secretaryship altho
> the duties are not that of the average
> secretary. Your time will be completely
> occupied for a period of several weeks,
> possibly longer.
>
> You will report to no one but me at my
> office, which by the way is an apartment in
> an exclusive downtown hotel.
>
> I am willing to pay you $100.00 per week and
> all expenses.

HASBEEN

SKETCH 8

```
If you are at liberty and think you would
care to help me in this unusual work, rather
than writing letters, interviewing clients,
answering telephone calls, etc., you may
consider yourself engaged."
```

It didn't take any time for reflection and I replied:

```
"I am already on your payroll; am unattached
and my undivided attention is yours from now
on. What's the nature of this commission."
```

Let us call her "Hasbeen" for short, even though she was the wife - in name at least - of one of Chicago's general utilities magnates.*

Hasbeen locked all doors and even drew curtains across the French windows before sinking into an easy chair and pouring into my ears a strange story of her husband's peculiarities.

```
"My dear' she said 'I am a most unhappy
woman. After twenty-five years of marital
bliss some strange phenomena have taken
possession of my husband.
     'He is no longer interested in anything
concerning me, hasn't spent an evening here
in a year; he seems oblivious to everything
```

---

* "Hasbeen" is most likely Margaret Anna Bird (1873-1953), the popular stage actress who went by the name Gladys Wallis and was the wife of the president of Commonwealth Edison, Samuel Insull (1859-1938).

pertaining to home, in fact, with the
exception of a few remarks at dinner he
rarely speaks at all. This state of affairs
is driving me wild and I must know what he
does every night between the hours of eight
and midnight. It is a fact that he is at his
office during these hours but unless I can
find out just what he does there night after
night I shall lose my mind.

'Now I have lived with Mr. Mack too many
years not to know that in his earlier and
busier years an evening conference was a
rare occurrence. We dine as always at seven,
usually in silence, and up until a few months
ago he would hurry through the meal, say
something about an evening conference and
rush out to his car.

'Lately at the dinner hour he places
his old-fashioned watch on the table, sips
at his soup, tastes the entree and roast,
lights a cigarette and is gone, without any
explanation.

'Mr. Mack is Vice-President of a great
utilities corporation, with heads of the many
departments to care for all detail; there
isn't the slightest reason for business worry
and of course conferences every night are
absurdities."

Hasbeen drained her highball, mixed two more placing one
before me, and with a long, dreary sigh, continued:

"We used to have such good times; belonged
to smart clubs and enjoyed social affairs;
he liked good music and we never missed the
opera, but that is all of the past and now
I'm alone.

'Mr. Mack has never been what anyone would
call a ladies man; he always used to say that
a man who played around with petticoats was
a fool - that women made all the trouble in
the world. Nevertheless I had him followed
for a long time recently to ascertain if
there might be a woman and the reports were
negligible; every minute was accounted for,
and with the exception of the driving time to
and from the house he was at his office."

At this point, I lit a cigarette and puffed nervously while the old
girl raved on.

"Now what I have in mind for you to do
is to get into his private office in some
manner, and ascertain what so occupies him
with sufficient importance that it takes
four hours time every evening throughout the
year."

I asked Mrs. Mack how in the world I could do that and she
continued:

"Mr. Mack has a beautiful suite of offices
on the top floor of the _____

Building.* His private secretary, Miss
Stevens, has been with him for ten years and
is a very unattractive but efficient woman of
about thirty-five. She is a typical old maid
and supports an aged mother; she has grown
up with our business and although Mr. Mack
has often remarked that she does not fit into
the present surroundings nevertheless she is
almost indispensable to the organization; he
says she has the unheard of feminine virtue
of keeping her ears open and mouth shut.

'Miss Stevens' assistant, Miss Greer,
is of the same type, though younger, and
inasmuch as she was employed by Miss Stevens
is also an old fashioned girl.

'I am telling you this to put your mind at
rest as to any possible chance of feminine
attraction in this private office. As to
the general offices, any flirtation in that
direction would be impossible for a man in
the exalted position held by Mr. Mack."

Mrs. Mack took a silk and lace handkerchief from a table and dapped at both eyes for a moment or two as she bewailed something about missing him so. My better judgment told me to make any possible exit, but noticing my uneasiness Hasbeen continued:

* Insull's office was located in the eighteen-story Edison Building
at 72 West Adams Street, built in 1907 and designed by Daniel H.
Burnham and Co.

"As before stated, my husband has been
followed and there seems to be no other
woman, proven by the facts that he calls
nowhere, visits no cafes, is seen only with
men associates, comes directly home for seven
o'clock dinner and then again when he leaves
the office at midnight.

'I know the hours between eight and
midnight are spent in his office because
no matter when I telephone, after the
switchboard is disconnected for the night, he
answers himself.

'The few times I went to see him in the
evenings it was impossible to get in owing
to the locked doors and darkness of the outer
offices. A few months ago I mentioned calling
for him around midnight but this irritated
him; in fact I have completely lost him and
must find out why. You say you are ingenuous
and a chiseler, now can you help me?"

Mrs. Mack was really weeping and I was wondering about
the hundred dollars a week and expenses and after partaking
of the highball she had placed beside me at the start of our conversation, replied;

"My dear Mrs. Mack, just at the moment I
cannot give you a definite promise as to
results. This is a large order but I accept
your proposition and after a night's study

I would like to report to you tomorrow
definitely whether or not I can succeed."

"All right then, tomorrow at my apartment,
Rooms _____ Auditorium Annex, 11 A.M. I shall
expect your confidence as no one knows of
this hide-away place but myself and my maid,
who is absolutely loyal and has leased this
apartment under an assumed name. Just come
right up promptly at eleven."*

Disgusted and discouraged I walked home; the cool, crisp air from the lake was invigorating but why in the world should such idiotic jobs present themselves. If a man preferred to remain in his office rather than pass the time with a wife who refused to diet and make herself pleasant to look upon, well, why shouldn't he? Still the hundred dollars a week just to find out something wouldn't be difficult work and then, too, the thrill of adventure was worth something.

It was late and the kiddies were asleep; the apartment was quiet and after an hours relaxation in my comfy kimona - those days - decided upon my plan of procedure. I would determine just what Mr. Mack did in his office between eight and midnight but would insist upon five weeks salary in advance - no more Pierre check book stuff for me.

The next morning found me at the Annex and up to the proper suite of rooms at 11 A.M.

* The apartment was in the Auditorium Annex, the 1907 extension of the Auditorium Hotel (eventually the Congress Hotel), at 504 South Michigan Avenue. The annex was designed by Holabird and Roche.

Hasbeen was waiting for me, and alone. I explained to her my plan and she was so pleased that she readily wrote me a check for the $500.00.

When asked for an exact description of Miss Stevens, secretary to Mr. Mack, Hasbeen did this so vividly that there would be no mistaking anyone else for this capable person.

Mr. Mack's great office building was not far from the Annex, and my work began.

From noon until two o'clock I watched the lobby to see if I could locate Miss Stevens when she would probably leave for lunch. Not being successful in finding the lady, the second day found me at the same place on the lookout but without result; the third day I knew I had found her.

Miss Stevens was alone and I followed; she went into a little tea room just off the Boulevard. She looked weary as she wandered the length of the room apparently looking for a table where she could be alone. She stopped at a booth and was lost to me for a moment or so, but as I sauntered up to her table and asked if she were expecting someone she replied in the negative and we lunched across the table but without a word from either. During the luncheon I thought I caught a smile as her tired eyes would momentarily glance over the jostling crowds of diners. Finishing her repast she slowly picked up her check and left.

Almost every day she lunched at this little tea room and it took nearly a week before we became speaking acquaintances. She would always search an unoccupied table and it was quite a coincidence how we happened to locate the same table at the same time.

(SKETCH NINE)

MISS STEVENS

SKETCH 9

One day I told her how much I enjoyed seeing her at the luncheon hour, that I was a stranger in the city searching for a secretarial position, but had been unable to find one just to my liking due to the exceptional work I had been doing in Florida for almost five years.

To my surprise she replied that she looked forward mornings to one o'clock hoping to see me again at the tea room. She said she had lived in Chicago for ten years and knew no-one; that she became so lonely at times she was on the verge of suicide and were it not for an invalid mother dependent upon her for support she wouldn't care whether school kept or not. She told me she was doing secretarial work and would be glad to help me if she heard of anything worth while. Miss Stevens loitered over her coffee while she slowly chatted about work, her mother, the noise and grime of the city, the hope of a spring-time vacation amid rambling farm houses - green of gently sloping hills and flowering meadows, and the lyric songs of birds.

I walked back to her office building with her and we agreed to meet at luncheon the following day.

Ten days had gone by and my reports to Hasbeen had not conveyed the information she so much desired. She said I was making progress but couldn't understand why I had not asked Miss Stevens just what Mr. Mack did at the office in the evenings.

After assuring Mrs. Mack that before the five weeks advanced pay had been earned she would have the answer to her query and that time was a most essential element in obtaining absolute facts, she agreed to be patient. I told her how tired, worn and thin Miss Stevens appeared to be; of her invalid mother and of her lonliness, and of her wish to return to the simplicity of the country; and Hasbeen's Chinese eyes almost closed as she snapped out something about the inadvisability of Miss Stevens giving up her work and Mr. Mack obtaining a younger secretary.

I was instructed to take Miss Stevens to dinners and to shows and to spare no expense in an endeavor to make life easier and happier as Mrs. Mack did not want her to sever her connection with general utilities.

The next day at luncheon I asked Miss Stevens if she would care to attend a performance of Rose Marie with me at a local theatre; that I had purchased tickets cheap from a scalper and didn't want to go alone. She said she would be delighted and would meet me about six o'clock and we could have dinner at the Russian Tea Room before going to the theatre.*

At dinner that evening Miss Stevens and I became friends. I followed her line of thought and it wasn't long before her office became the topic of conversation.

She said she didn't like her chief, Mr. Mack, but she was too old to fit in anywhere else and it would be impossible to obtain another connection at her splendid salary. She said he had been a very active person and was possessed of an unusually brilliant mind; that up until a couple of years ago they were swamped with work but now, since the organization of the new Company with its great building and many departments, the office of the Vice-President was relieved of so much of it's former detail that Mr. Mack had little to do and as a consequence had become restless and irritable at times.

```
Secretary    - "You never have to work nights
               then, do you?"
```

* *Rose-Marie*, an operetta by Czech composer Rudolf Friml, was the longest running Broadway musical of the 1920s.

Miss Stevens – "No, thank goodness, we really
could close our private offices
about four in the afternoon but Mr.
Mack remains in his room until six
and I do not like to leave before
he does."

Secretary   – "That isn't very thoughtful of him,
is it? If your work is finished and
he is not busy it would seem as
though he would at least quit at
five o'clock if for no other reason
than to make your day an hour
shorter."

Miss Stevens – "Yes, thats true, but he don't seem
to ever want to go home. I don't
think his domestic life is over-
joyous; his wife used to phone him
at all hours of the day, for no
reason at all, and it annoyed him.
'I have been with him for ten
years, the first four or five of
which she would drive to the office
about four o'clock and sit in the
car and wait for him to go home.
He would make her wait longer and
longer until finally she ceased
calling; now she never phones or
calls and I have an idea they are
none too happy."

Secretary   - "Is she pretty?"

Miss Stevens - "No. I never liked her looks or
               her manner; he used to keep a
               photograph on his desk, taken about
               the time they were married and she
               was fairly attractive then, but
               that picture passed from sight long
               ago. She's fat, blonde and whiny,
               you know the type."

A pretty little waitress in Russian costume brought us some hot tea in tall glasses and dainty monogrammed cigarettes. It was almost time to leave for the theatre and our conversation drifted to modern life, Florida, Pierre, green hedges and blue mountains, vacations, musical comedies and Strange Interlude.*

Miss Stevens told me she never went to a moving picture, she considered them cheap and commonplace but she did appreciate good music and had been told that the melodies of Rose Marie were exceptionally symphonic; she appreciated the invitation to the theatre and hoped she might repay the courtesy soon. She said she was so tired, and hungry for a place to laze under big sheltering trees and enjoy life through the contemplation of nature, that the apple trees were now in bloom and she longed to take her mother to the country for a two week's springtime vacation.

During the intermissions at the theatre we again talked of our secretarial experiences. I told her I had about lost hope of finding suitable work in Chicago and was elated when she

* *Strange Interlude*, first produced in 1928, is a long and formally innovative play by Eugene O'Neill that deals frankly with sexuality.

thought it might be possible for me to substitute for her if she were sufficiently fortunate to be granted a two weeks leave so early in the season. She said she would suggest the idea to Mr. Mack in the morning, and it might work out although the usual procedure was assistance from the general offices.

My enthusiasm at the prospect of two weeks work in her office was overwhelming and she did not object to my proposed visit to her office just before lunch time on the morrow.

After the show and au revoirs I wanted to phone Hasbeen and report the splendid progress but decided it was too late; it would be better to wend my way toward home with the knowledge that I carried horse-shoes in both pockets.

The following Monday I became temporary secretary to Mr. Mack; he had been glad to permit Miss Stevens a two weeks vacation and to allow me to take her place.

Miss Greer, assistant to Miss Stevens, was at her desk when I arrived. With the exception of the two desks, one of which was assigned to me, the attractive but small office contained only the usual file cabinets, safe, chairs and a table. After introductions and instructions she said inasmuch as Mr. Mack had not yet arrived she would show me his office adjoining ours. She added that no one except the President of the Company, who was living in New York but visited Chicago frequently, ever entered Mr. Mack's office without first conferring with Miss Stevens, and that she was not permitted to knock on his door but compelled to use their private speaking tube before she or anyone else could gain entrance. Miss Greer told me that Mr. Mack was very particular about this; that he did not like to be disturbed and for me not to worry if he did not answer the speaking tube when I called; that he knew he was wanted and would ring back when he wished to do so.

She showed me Mr. Mack's office, a sumptuous one and elegant with its furnishings of unfinished walnut. It was larger and better equipped than the average office but otherwise there was nothing unusual about the room.

Shortly after Mr. Mack arrived, smiled and nodded as he passed our desks and entered his office. During the morning he sent for me to take dictation, the usual straight business communications.

I thought he was very nice and wondered why Miss Stevens didn't like him. When I would call him he was courtesy itself and to me he was a real executive.

Whether or not Mr. Mack liked my work he told me he was pleased and wished his two assistants had my background - whatever that means. I tried to handle the work as I thought Miss Stevens would do and enjoyed the position, often wishing that I were working only for Mr. Mack and not for his wife.

Noticing a door in his office opposite the entry to our office I asked Miss Greer where that door led to as Mr. Mack frequently used that door to enter what appeared to be a hallway. She said no one knew that they thought it was his private rest room but no one but Mr. Mack or the President ever opened that door.

Taking some letters in for his signature, during Mr. Mack's absence, I managed enough courage to open the personal door; a frightened, quick glance rewarded me nothing but a long narrow passageway.

My reports to Hasbeen were now made between one and two o'clock, my lunch hour. She would order a salad and coffee brought to her suite for me, but her disappointment over my unsatisfactory reports chilled my eagerness for even that delectable dish and stimulant.

I told her of Mr. Mack's phone calls, his correspondence and his callers, of the time of arrival and departure; there was nothing to discover but ordinary office routine.

She evinced great interest regarding my night visits to the office; how about nine P.M. on two occasions I had unlocked the door to the outer office, made my way slowly and quietly through the semi-darkness to Miss Stevens' office and kept watch for sometime. There was a light in his office but the door was closed and nothing was visible through the frosted glass; apparently he was alone for there was not a sound. I told her of my fear of being discovered and of my alibi in such a predicament, viz., just happened to be downtown, it was cool and stopped in for my coat, thoughtlessly forgotten when leaving the office at six o'clock. She seemed pleased at my report of how after leaving the office I had entered a nearby drug store, called the office and when hearing his voice say "Hello" had hung up the receiver.

The first weeks work was completed and when Mr. Mack asked me to draw checks for Miss Greer and myself saying he would sign them my conscience bothered me - I was being paid by both the Macks and my strict Presbyterian training didn't quite approve. I asked Hasbeen what her idea was of that and she said not to give a thought about the money, that I was holding down two jobs and entitled to double wages; but to spend more of my time thinking about what I had promised to do for her.

One week more before Miss Stevens' return necessitated some deep mental activity.

Mr. Mack couldn't spend those hours reading as there were no books around; it was evident he didn't play solitaire as I had looked for a deck of cards and found none; he didn't study stocks and bonds as no charts, pocket manuels or market printed clippings were in sight; he wasn't a race track fan for if so uncashed tickets or entry lists would be scattered about. Something told me to investigate that secret door more thoroughly.

Wednesday of my last week at the office found me no nearer to the solution of Hasbeen's problem and I was truly discouraged when Mr. Mack advised me that the President of the Company would be with us tomorrow for Miss Greer had informed me that he occupied Mr. Mack's office when in Chicago; there would be no chance to examine the long hallway.

Thursday morning found me more smartly dressed than usual with a marcel and manicure - in other words at my best. The President arrived on schedule, a prominent New Yorker who had a mailing address at the Hoffman House.*

Mr. Mack and I were answering the morning mail when the President walked in; he smoked incessantly as he listened to the dictation, now and then making a criticism or a commendation. He finally dropped into one of the luxurious leather and walnut arm chairs and embarrassed me very much by his quizzing glances in my direction. I remembered how and when I had met him before but didn't flatter myself that he could possibly recall such a casual acquaintance. Mr. Mack was called from the office for a few moments and the following conversation took place:

---

* The president of the company was Thomas A. Edison (1847-1931), the most prolific inventor in American history, who over his lifetime recorded 1,093 patents.

President   –   "You know its strange but surely we
                  have met before – I rarely forget a
                  face and am positive this is not our
                  first introduction."

Secretary   –   "Yes, I remember you very well; it
                  was not so long ago when you were
                  vacationing in the land of tropic
                  magic. Do you remember a palace
                  on the shores of Biscayne Bay with
                  its marble facades and gasping with
                  luxury and beauty?"

President   –   "You mean Florida? 'Why, yes, but
                  where did we meet, were you at The
                  Breakers, The Roney-Plaza – surely
                  not at Beau's Eden?

Secretary   –   "Your last guess is correct – I saw
                  you first in the east loggia as you
                  were looking out to sea and enjoying
                  the foreigness, friendliness, beauty
                  and happiness of Beau's Paradise."

President   –   "You were his secretary – yes, I
                  remember, – but what in the world
                  are you doing in this wild city after
                  that enchanting environment. What
                  are you doing here – is Miss Stevens'
                  pensioned?"

Secretary - "Why no, of course not. She is on a
vacation and I am substituting for
her. My work will be over tomorrow
or Saturday and I'm sorry because I
enjoy the work here very much. Mr.
Mack has been very nice to me and
considerate in overlooking my many
blunders."

President - "Maybe I can fix it up for you; he
isn't keen about Miss Stevens any
more; there was a time when she
was very valuable to our Company
but now, as you can see, what this
office requires is a secretary of
poise, dignity and beauty as well as
capability."

(Secretary smiles)

Secretary - "Do you think I could fill that
bill."

President - "One-hundred percent."

Secretary - "Thanks so much but I am engaged
on other work beginning Monday at
which time Miss Stevens will return
here."

(President smokes and smiles. Secretary also smiles)

President   - "Would like awfully well to have you
               join me at luncheon today. Now don't
               say no, say yes."

(Enters Mr. Mack)

President   -
to Mr. Mack "Well you're a selfish brute; why
             didn't you tell me we had acquired
             Beau Brummel's private secretary to
             teach us refinement?"

(Mr. Mack looks at Secretary and both laugh)

Mr. Mack   - "Thought it best not, but it didn't
               take me long to approve Miss Stevens'
               suggestion and regret the work is of
               such short duration."

President   -
to Mr. Mack "I have asked Miss _____ to have
             lunch with me today but she hasn't
             accepted as yet; she hasn't said no
             either so I'm telling you that we
             will join you and Florence at one
             o'clock.

(Mr. Mack turned, jerked his head, and stared at
the President.)
(Secretary hurriedly left the room)

What the President and the Vice-President of this great organization discussed after I left their private office I do not know,

but before the morning was over the President stopped at my desk and in an undertone said "Not a word to anyone but Mr. Macks office at one o'clock." I smiled and in assent.

(SKETCH TEN)*

When opportunity presented I left the office, rushed to a telephone booth in soda shop on main floor, and phoned Hasbeen to advise her of luncheon with the President and her husband at one. She suggested asking the President what her husband did at the office every evening and I assured her only two days remained to ferret out this puzzle and I did not intend to fall down on the job.

Promptly at one o'clock I took my finished work into Mr. Mack's office. My eyebrows seemed to rise an inch as I faced three cocktail glasses filled to the brim standing on his desk. The President handed one to me, then one to Mr. Mack, and the last to himself as he gave a rather risque toast about happy rendezvous. He said it wouldn't be necessary to get my wraps, that a surprise awaited me and to prepare myself for a repast such as Oscar might place before me at the Waldorf.†

The President led the way to the mysterious door and we three went down that long, weird passageway and up a circular stair, at the top of which he opened another door and as we en-

---

* If this drawing is, in fact, of Thomas Edison, it depicts him at a much younger age, since in 1922 Edison was seventy-five years old.
† Oscar Tschirky was the beloved maître d'hôtel at the Waldorf Astoria Hotel in New York.

THE PRESIDENT

SKETCH 10

tered it seemed as though I had instantaneously emerged from a secretary to Alice in Wonderland.*

Before me was a home; a living room luxurious in its appointments with tempting vista of dining room and sunporch beyond. It seemed impossible that up on the roof of one of Chicago's big business blocks could be a home, bungalow or apartment, and especially a secret place accessible to one of the cities greatest offices. Nevertheless there it was, and probably still is, with however a change in occupants.

A colored maid brought in another round of cocktails, only this time there were four glasses on the tray.

Bewildered in my astonishment I do not recall the words passed between the President and Mr. Mack, but coming towards us from somewhere was a lovely vision in white. Aphrodite could not have impressed the old Romans more than this enchanting creature thrilled me; she seemed a combination of springtime flowers - white and pink of cherryblossoms, delicacy of lillies, sweetness of jasmine, freshness of violets and with gayety of an old fashioned garden.

Nita had been an Iris, Babs a wild rose, but here was an orchid.

They introduced her simply as Florence.

(SKETCH ELEVEN)

Florence was very gracious as she smiled and offerred her hand, saying how nice it was of me to join them at luncheon. She was so poised, so calm and cool, and so adorably sweet as she asked that we join her in a cocktail before luncheon, that

---

* There are no extant drawings of the top floors of the Edison Building and nothing to confirm that there was, in fact, such a space.

FLORENCE

SKETCH 11

my glass was raised with the others in silent toast to her lovliness.

During the luncheon the President and Mr. Mack shared a bottle of champagne. I guess they absorbed more bubbles than they anticipated inasumch as they discussed the advisability of postponing an important meeting scheduled for that afternoon. They decided to drive out to the plant, and Mr. Mack asked Florence to take me to a matinee, adding that Miss Greer could manage the office detail.

After the gentlemen disappeared down the circular stair Florence said we would have a few moments to indulge in the luxury of idleness and relaxation before going to the show.

She asked me where I lived and when the location and apartment were described she laughed and said we were neighbors, that she and her mother had an apartment close by.

Florence inquired as to my stay in Mr. Mack's office and when informed that my work would be finished on the morrow, she said she was so glad because inasmuch as I knew the President the four of us could have happy times when he was in the city.

I told her my evenings were usually spent with my two children and how happy I would be were she to favor me with a visit some evening.

Florence laughed and said she didn't believe a word of it, that I was too young and if I were mother and wife what was I doing in the business world.

I told her of being alone with Tidbits, of Nita and Blossom and how difficult it was to find secretarial work if one were truthful as to married status.

Florence became very serious as she listened to my story and then seemed relieved to speak of her experiences. She had been

the wife of a South Water street merchant,* a man twice her age;
the marriage had been arranged by her mother and the first few
months were fairly happy ones travelling in foreign lands but
after returning to Chicago her husband spent all his time at his
work and she was left too much alone. Finally a son was born
but only to live a few hours, following which event she sought
forgetfulness in the less serious life of a big city.

She spoke of meeting Mr. Mack several years before and
that from that introduction a sincere friendship had come into
being; and for the past two years they had been devoted to one
another.

Our conversation continued:

```
Secretary  - "What became of your husband and Mr.
             Mack's wife?"


Florence   - "My husband and I agreed to disagree
             and we obtained a divorce about the
             time this big office building was
             completed. Since then mother and
             I have our apartment where I sleep
             and have my breakfast but my happy
             hours are spent here in this home in
             the sky. Don't you think its lovely
             up here - so quiet, so restful and
             secluded?
             'Yes, Mr. Mack is married but his
             wife knows nothing of this rendezvous.
```

* South Water Street, on the banks of the Chicago River, was the
center of wholesale market activity in Chicago from the 1850s until
the early years of the twentieth century.

In fact we were seeing so much of each other that he had this cozy place designed and finished with the completion of the building, in order to shield his wife from idle gossip."

Secretary - "Oh, I'm so thrilled; this is more interesting than a show - do tell me how to find such companionship; a man as serious, kindly and dignified as Mr. Mack; I envy you this friendship but wouldn't you be still happier if Mrs. Mack did know and divorced him; then, maybe you would have a real home of your own?"

Florence - "No, I don't think so; some phases of married life are very distasteful to me; I much prefer the anticipation of meetings and the au revoirs of courtship to the possession of matrimony. It is so much fun to see him afternoons and evenings and then wonder what he is doing the rest of the time."

Secretary - "How in the world do you get in here. I have never seen you pass through the office."

(Florence laughs, lights a cigarette, and rings for the maid to bring in some Apricot Brandy)

Florence   - "Now wouldn't you like to know.
              In a few minutes I'm going to take
              you down in my very own electric
              elevator; it will land you in an
              alley entrance, no where near the
              lobby of the building."

Secretary   - "Do you dine here alone every
              evening?"

Florence   - "No, Mr. Mack always has dinner with
              me and we have our evenings together
              here leaving about midnight in our
              cars for home. He departs through
              his office and down the building
              elevators to his car and I use my
              own elevator and walk a block to the
              garage where my roadster is waiting.
              Mr. Mack joins his wife at seven
              o'clock dinner, where he says he has
              appetizers, then leaves promptly
              to join me at our later dinner. He
              always lights the light in his office
              as he passes through."

(Secretary laughing)

Secretary   - "Well I've heard of lots of
              strange friendships but this one is
              paramount. Suppose his wife were to

call him on the telephone while he is
supposed to be working in his office,
how would he explain the failure to
answer the phone."

Florence   - "There wouldn't be any failure.
Here, try this Apricot Brandy, its
deliciously smooth.
Mr. Mack has arranged so that the
phone rings here after he leaves his
office. A few nights ago someone
called about 9:30 but hung up when he
said "Hello". No one calls me here
and he said she probably rung up to
see if he were working. He says she
used to be curious as to what he
did at his office every evening but
lately she asks no questions. Come
on, we'll be late if we don't
hurry."

Secretary - I must go back to the office to get
my hat and coat. Thats funny, Miss
Greer will wonder why I've been in
Mr. Mack's office when he is out."

Florence   - "Better leave them there and wear
some of mine; I have a partial
wardrobe here. Why not come back
after the matinee and dine with us,

                    then you can get your things after
                    every one has gone for the day."

    Secretary   -   "Well, all right, but Miss Greer
                    will think it strange I went to lunch
                    without hat or coat and didn't even
                    phone."

    Florence   -   "Forget it - here's a pretty little
                    turban that will just match your
                    smart frock and this jacket will do -
                    its warm today."

Florence and I passed through another hallway and a small electric elevator took us to the ground. It seemed strange to pass through an alley but this entire transaction had been a series of unexpected events and a few more might be expected.

It was nice when the curtain was drawn back and the play started. Florence became quiet, apparently entranced with the plot or the actors. My eyes and ears saw and heard nothing but the grey matter in my brain was working overtime - what was I to do now - this was the fourth week of my work for Hasbeen - had accomplished what I started out to do but what a jam I was in at the moment. How could I tell her of this lovely girl by my side - her only fault was the urge for happiness away from the conservatism of a wretched world - if I were to report the facts three people instead of one would be miserable and that one's present distress would be intensified; it wouldn't help matters so far as Hasbeen was concerned for at present she knew where her husband was all of the time and enjoyed seeing and knowing he was home at least part of the day and night - and, too, Florence was so young and so divinely lovely sooner or later she probably would find companionship with a chap nearer her age - no, it would be wiser not to tell Mrs. Mack of her husband's infidelity.

At the conclusion of the performance I asked Florence to please permit me to decline her kind invitation to dinner - that the kiddies would be so disappointed - and if she didn't mind I would leave her turban and jacket in Mr. Mack's office in the morning. Assuring her that her secret was perfectly safe with me, thanking her for luncheon and the afternoon's entertainment, and wishing her all the luck in the world I left her and hurried toward State Street.

The department stores were about to close for the day but I managed to get to the toy department and purchase a slate pencil and slate before the clerk left his counter. On Wabash Avenue a book store was still open and I purchased a copy of a late edition.

My last morning at the office found me the first arrival. Noticing my coat and hat on the rack where I had left them the day before I rushed into Mr. Mack's office and arranged Florence's jacket and turban on a chair. Nearing Mr. Mack's walnut desk I placed the book and slate, purchased the evening before, thereon; a moment later I lifted them, took the articles to my office and carefully wrapped and deposited them near my wraps.

The morning passed quickly and a letter addressed to Miss Stevens was left on her desk, thanking her for the engagement and hoping to meet soon at our tea-room standby.

With the usual goodbyes and well wishes my business connection with general utilities was finished and I slowly wended my way to the last interview with Mrs. Mack.

Hasbeen was at her temporary office and alone; when I entered she was pacing up and down the length of the room with her characteristic stride and whiffing away at her constant cigarette.

I asked if she wouldn't please be seated, that while she didn't need to tell me what a disappointment I had been still there were some reports I wished to make.

She finally composed herself and waited for me to speak.

Secretary - "Mrs. Mack I have been in your employ four weeks and my work is finished. I am returning to you $100.00 the fifth week's advanced pay which is unearned. During the time I was in your husband's office I know there was never a telephone call except on business, never a feminine caller and every letter mailed has been a business communication.

'From what I have ascertained Mr. Mack's nightly visits are not concerned with his duties of Vice-President.

'He is not a reader, a follower of stocks and bonds, a race track fan or a player of cards.

'I am positive that not a soul enters his private office after six

o'clock, excepting of course the
cleaners of the building.

'You really have a wonderful
husband and should cease being
suspicious, try to forget worry and
become youthful once more. Probably
he is as lonely as you are.

'I am leaving you with a book
and a slate I took from his desk
this morning and through them
it is possible you will find the
solution to your problem. Perhaps
you remember what you told me in our
first interview as you spoke of some
strange phenomena having possession
of your husband; Mrs. Mack, to your
knowledge has he ever been interested
in spiritualism, believing that he
could commune with departed souls?"*

Mrs. Mack — "No — he always ridiculed anything of
that nature. I visit a trance medium
regularly and always have, but he
never had any faith in a hereafter
let alone receiving any messages from
beings not cognizable by the senses."

* Spiritualism is the belief that spirits from the dead can communi-
cate with the living, and even impart otherworldly wisdom to their
loved ones on Earth.

Secretary - "Is it possible for one in a trance
to receive written messages."

Mrs. Mack - "Certainly. A medium receiving
messages is in a state in which the
soul seems to pass out of the body,
a hypnotic condition, and has the
power to converse, through guides,
with loved ones in spirit life. It
is so satisfying to ask questions and
receive advice from those we knew
and cared for while they were with us
here on earth."

Secretary - "Do students of the occult spend
hours alone seeking spiritualistic
manifestations?"

Mrs. Mack - "I have heard that true spiritualists
commune in solitude for hours,
usually at night."

Secretary - "Here is the book and the strange
slate I lifted from your husband's
desk this morning."

Hasbeen examined them carefully and then gave me a
friendly pat on the shoulder simply saying "Thank you." I expressed my appreciation of her generosity and assured her of
my confidence.

The book was one written by Sir Arthur Conan Doyle, and on the slate was scrawled

"INDIAN GUIDE SAY YOUR OWN FAULT
SHE INDIFFERENT BECAUSE YOU
NOT HOME ENOUGH"*

* *

---

* Sir Arthur Conan Doyle (1859–1930), best known as the creator of the Sherlock Holmes mysteries, also was a spiritualist, and used proceeds from sales of his Holmes stories to fund speaking tours about spiritualism, including ones in 1921 and 1922 that included Chicago.

PHYLANDER & COMPANY

My next engagement was a long and happy one as secretary to a partner of Phylander & Company, members of the Chicago Board of Trade.*

It was nice to be in real business and my "Big Boss" here was one of the grandest men I have ever known - young, handsome, pleasant, practical but with an appreciation of beauty, kindly and generous. He had only one hobby, and whether stocks were selling long or short, golf took precedent. I told him of Tidbits as he appeared so genuinely human, and he was one of the few real executives I have met who was big enough to think it possible for a clever and capable secretary to be also a mother.

The work with this Company was very interesting, buying and selling stocks and bonds. The hours were short - nine until two - and what a treat it was to do a day's work and be home for an hour or two with the children before dinner time. Blossom was still with us but now that generous monthly checks were received from Nita's insurance policy, at Dr. Lerner's suggestion I was investigating some splendid girl's boarding schools in the

---

* "Phylander & Co." is a lightly disguised Raymond, Pynchon & Co., stockbrokers based in New York with offices in London and Chicago. In this chapter and elsewhere in the manuscript, Altemus handwrote the name "Phylander" over the typed name "Pynchon."

suburbs with the idea of placing Blossom among little girls of her age where she would be happy and receive the proper training.

It is real fun to be independent and earn one's way when business association and home environment are harmonious.

One evening Babs came in with tears in her eyes. She was to be operated on tomorrow, Saturday; she was afraid and nervous and said her husband was very angry - he didn't think it necessary that she be cut up but Dr. Lerner knew it was imperative: would I please go to the hospital with her and watch the operation.

We didn't keep open office on Saturday mornings; it was summer and the week's work was concluded on Friday, so I told Babs she could count on me helping her to the hospital but as to watching an operation I would promise nothing.

Babs and I arrived at the Ravenswood Hospital about 8:30 A.M. and the nurses gave me a white apron and cap. I held Bab's hand and before they administered the chloroform she told me she was happy that the Doctor was going to cut her up. She laughed and joked as long as she could and I knew by the twinkle in her eyes that she was glad to have me near.

It was horrible but fascinating to watch Dr. Lerner, his two assistants and the two nurses, cut, clamp, tie, scrape and sew up Bab's anatomy. She was talking and laughing; then she told a little story about the Doctor but no one except myself was listening.

In about a half an hour the operation seemed to be completed as Dr. Lerner glanced over at me and asked if he might talk with me a minute. We walked a short distance from the others and he said;

"Babs needs a second operation, a serious

```
operation, will you kindly go downstairs
and telephone her husband at once and ask
his permission. If he does not approve we
will go no further but I advise this be done
immediately."
```

Calling the tailor shop Babs husband heard my message and seemed cross as he replied;

```
"You tell Dr. Lerner for me that I know
no reason for, don't approve of and am not
paying for any operations. Tell him I said he
seems to know more about my wife's troubles
than I do and to use his own judgment; tell
him to cut her heart out for all I care."
```

I had never liked Babs husband and after those few words cancelled him from my knowing list. I told the Doctor just what he said with the exception of cutting out the heart remark.

Dr. Lerner told his assistants to administer another ether, after which Babs remained perfectly still while they started all over again with the cutting process. I felt sick but knew there was no way for me to leave the room without disturbing the others and I must stick it out - the doctors and nurses had bandages of some sort over their mouths and noses, but they had failed to provide one for me and the inhaled fumes of chloroform and ether were making me dizzy.

It was a long operation and when finally completed and Babs was in a room downstairs I told the Doctor how miserable I felt and wanted to get a taxi and go home. He said Babs would be in extreme pain when she came out of the ether and if I could possibly remain to please do so. He cautioned me about advising her of her husband's remarks and said I would feel better in a little while.

When Babs did come to her senses she screamed with pain and begged me to find the Doctor and have him come to her. He did and after long deliberation told the nurses to give her a hypodermic whenever the pain became too great.

After giving Babs a shot of something in the arm and she became quiet the nurse told me Babs would sleep for a long time and for me to go if I wished.

It was luncheon time when I arrived at our apartment and the aroma from the kitchen didn't help me a bit. Margaret made me a cup of tea and then told me how Babs' husband with three men had removed all the furniture from their apartment and big vans carried it away. She said the apartment was vacant, that he had paid Babs' maid and she, too, had gone.

I told Margaret to clean out Nita's room - that Babs would need it when her hospital time was through.

Three weeks later Babs became a member of our household; her husband had left but agreed to send her a weekly allowance. She said it was all for the best - that she still believed in progression and one couldn't be a tailor's wife more than three years.

Almost a year passed pleasantly with Phylander & Company and what a delightful group of people they were.

Mr. Phylander, whose office was in New York, frequently spent a day or two in the Chicago branch.

On one of his visits a wire came for him as he sat in our office. Handing it to him he read the message and said:

```
"I must take the Century
to New York. Mrs. Phylander
is seriously ill."
```

The day following he and I shared a common sorrow - his wife in New York City, and my father in a little town in Illinois - had suddenly passed away.*

* * * * * * * * * * * * * * * * * * * *

---

* Altemus's father, Charles J. McDowell, died in Elgin, Illinois, on May 27, 1923 at age sixty-one from "a hemorrhage of the left lung" brought on by asthma, from which he had suffered for twenty years.

COUNTRY

September of 1924 rolled around. Tidbits had frolicked into his seventh year and my twenty-<u>seventh</u> anniversary was just around the corner.*

Our tiny playmate, Blossom, was no longer a member of our household; she was enjoying life in an exclusive children's school just outside of Chicago. To say Tidbits missed his little pal would be to lack judgment in the choice of verbs - he grieved for her.

Babs, too, had left us; she progressed to the Drake Hotel.†

Following my father's passing I had resigned from Phylander & Company; Tidbits and I were getting old and we wanted to visit the country and see the horses, cows, silos, haystacks and all the other things we read about in story books. Giving up the apartment and with farewells to faithful Margaret we left for a vacation not very far away.

Forty miles northwest of the Windy City on the banks of the beautiful Fox River lies the quiet little town of Elgin, sometimes

---

* In September of 1924, Althea would have really been thirty-eight and Robert almost eleven.
† The Drake Hotel, located on the southeast corner of North Michigan Avenue and East Lake Shore Drive, was an elegant, high-end hotel with accompanying residential suites.

called Bluff City due to the steep banks on both sides of the stream.

Although the inhabitants feel that their village is one of sophistication and modernity, to me it is just a charming place where one can forget the clamorous staccato voice of the city, the bark of auto horns, blurred musical intonations of newsboys, saxophones and radios.

Elgin is cool in summer with its great elm, maple and mammoth oaks shading the funny old red brick pavements and concrete and tar sidewalks; with its parks between slopes of ravines; with its many lakes and lagoons and with its great fountain in the heart of town spraying cooling water to quench parched palates of humans and animals alike.

(SKETCH TWELVE)

In this quaint community with its friendly hills and sunny valleys, Tidbits and I had several weeks play, visiting with mother, grandmother and cousins, just loafing, fishing, canoeing and swimming. We were gathering water lillies while paddling around in a canoe on the river one day when I told Tidbits this town was my birthplace and asked him if he liked it. He said he wished he could stay in the country with grandma, that he didn't want to go back to a city and he didn't see why I couldn't find work there as well as in a big place. I told him there were no "big bosses" in little towns who needed private secretaries, but that if he could do without me maybe I would go to New York for a while.

Before our sojourn was over it was decided that Tidbits would linger with his grandma and enter school and that I have a chance at real secretaryship in a real city - New York. It would

FOX RIVER

SKETCH 12

be my first separation from my inspiration and it didn't appeal but I had chosen a business career and when one has reached the age of twenty-seven it wouldn't do to fall down on the job. And, too, as soon as I could arrange for him he could be placed on the Limited and travel the eighteen hour journey in safety.

Saying goodbye to Tidbits was a heartbreak but after a few hours on the train I was catching tantalizing vistas of strange bits of architecture, hodge-podge of house fronts stained by time and paints in tints of green, blue and white, sleepy quaint villages, smoke filled cities, vast geometric patterns of corn, rye and wheat and great glittering rivers.

The journey was interesting on the second day when we came into the higher altitudes of cooler air where cloud tufts would swim below and occasionally veil the slow-changing panorama of earth beneath - mountains passing and then falling abruptly away - rivers wandering whimsically through valleys and across lowlands intervening between hilly ranges - then, Washington, Philadelphia and all too soon New York.

NEW YORK

Stepping from the Limited and feeling the first flush of ex-
citement in the rush of humanity, the hum of taxicabs, husky
voices of the redcaps and the deep baying of whistles exhila-
rated me to the sense of well being, but never shall I forget the
loneliness and homesickness of those first days in New York.

Like all nice girls I registered at the Martha Washington
Hotel.*

Here I met Jetta Goudal. She had just arrived from France
and spoke of losing her fiance in the war and was in America to
sell some scenarioes she had written. All the temperament one
reads about in the Movie Magazines must have developed after
she left the Martha Washington, for at that time she was a perfectly sane, adorable and frugal maiden.

I think its just splendid the exotic Jetta was awarded
$37,000.00 recently in a suit against Cecil de Mille for the last
time I saw her was in Lord & Taylors, where she was purchasing some little piece of chintz to brighten up the windows of her
small bedroom in the aforesaid hostelry. Jetta must have been
very puritanical at that time as she refused to dine anywhere

* The Martha Washington Hotel, at 29 East Twenty-Ninth Street, was
the first hotel built in New York to provide housing for working
women.

except in said hotel - if any boy friends insisted on taking her
to dinner they either had to console themselves with the grille
and lobby of the Martha Washington or else they just didn't eat
or woo at all.*

Several business women living at the hotel advised me that
it was almost impossible for an out-of-towner to find secretarial
work in New York in a big way, and that it was unheard of for a
non-college girl to obtain anything beyond a stenographic job,
to say nothing of a Mrs. with an offspring. This didn't curb my
enthusiasm one whit and to the College Bureau I went to file
an application. I would take my chance with lies and then more
lies. I would be a Miss again and a graduate of one of the countries best universities.

A perusal of the application I filled out should have brought
secretaryship to the President of the United States. A searching
of my prevarications on this document would have been disas-
trous, but most any secretary knows that if she can get by first
interviews and secure the work, the chances are slim for later
investigations of that hated application blank.

Apparently I had made an impression - there was an opening in New York no agency had been able to fill. They said the
gentleman was a crank and not only demanded efficiency, college background and knowledge of French, but also youth,
beauty, poise and an unbobbed brunette.

The youth and beauty requisites had me bothered a bit, but
I always had a monumental regard for a go-getter and I didn't
intend to let youth and beauty stand in the way.

* Jetta Goudal (1891-1985), the stage name of Dutch-born Jewish actress Julie Henriette Goudeket, was a close friend of Marion Davies.
After director Cecil B. DeMille fired her for what he called a "tem-
peramental outburst," she sued DeMille and won a $31,000 settlement
in 1929.

An interview was arranged with the gentleman and we talked about everything but business. I told him of Beau's Eden and he said he was crazy about Florida, said he could hardly wait until he could get back there to fish. He did look at the application blank and then asked when I would be available and at what salary.

The following Monday was my business debut in the Metropolis. I became private secretary to an organizer of the cities most exclusive clubs.*

This "Big Boss" was the most nervous man I have ever known; to keep him in lead pencils would be an extravagance for the average office as he could devour at least half a dozen each morning. He didn't smoke, but to say he didn't chew would be adding to my list of untruths, because after hanging up his hat and stick the first duty was to grab one of the six newly sharpened pencils and start to bite. Before twenty minutes that poor piece of wood looked like a corrugated tapeworm and the second woodbound lead was on its way.

Now this gentleman was fond of poetry. It seems his first wife had been quite a romantic soul and during her married life had each day written a new poem for her dear husband. After her death he had all the poems printed and bound into a one and only volume. Now that he taken unto himself a second bride, this pretty little green and gold book had a secret cubbyhole in his desk at the office.

Poems were the first business of the day. We would read them together and my commendations of certain ones and eulogies

* This "big boss" is likely Harry S. Black (1863-1930), the chairman of the U.S. Realty and Improvement Corporation (USRIC), owner of several hotels, including the Plaza, and a prominent New York social club promoter.

over the creative imagination of others pleased him immensely. These poetic conceptions started our day beautifully and would have been all to the good but he had a very bad habit of scribbling snatches of poems all over the margins of business communications. It kept me busy checking all documents leaving his desk to keep them free of wood splinters and lovesick quibbles.

Our work in this office was to organize city, country, bath and tennis, beach and riding clubs. Through lists and memberships of existing exclusive associations we would pick out about twenty of the best known people and invite them - sometimes with bait - to serve on the Board of Governors of any new club we happened to be promoting.

In this way these socially or otherwise prominent humans obtained memberships valued from $5000.00 to $50,000.00 free of charge.

The poor social climbers, taking out and paying their hard earned cash for entree into said new club, fancied themselves as now becoming members of the four hundred, while as a matter of fact the original twenty would probably never see the clubhouse. However this was a prosperous racket for all concerned.

This "big boss" could never eat lunch. Whether his tummy had lead poisoning or not I do not know, but each day we had his noon-day repast brought in from a nearby hotel, and every days menu was a replica of the day preceding, viz., pint of milk and a few crackers. It was tiresome to see him munch on those dry, crisp pieces of dough, so one noon I brought back two delicious little chocolate cakes and placed them beside the milk and crackers. To my delight the cakes were consumed with what appeared to be ravishment; but the next day came the request for no more pastries - just crackers.

All went well with this secretaryship for about a year. Then one day this big boy appeared at the office in a state of exhaustion; his eyes were swollen from tears and he appeared a complete physical wreck. If ever a man needed a bracer now was the time, but outside of pencils, poems and forgetfulness he had no bad habits. He told me how his young wife had left him, leaving at home their year old baby. She had removed all negotiable securities from their safety deposit box, drawn all funds from checking accounts, bought a brand new roadster on his credit and had disappeared.

After a nervous breakdown this splendid Chief did not have the inspiration to promote more clubs, and as his mental anguish worried me too much, I resigned.*

* *

Before answering advertisements or visiting agencies relative to a new business connection, I decided to write to Enry Hay Hick's daughter Ellen, who was noted for her charities and benevolence.† Her mother's brother was my husband's uncle and he had lived with us in Philadelphia before Tidbits was born. It might be possible that she could refer me to someone in her social set needing a secretary.‡

I knew the futility of requesting any favors from Mrs. Hick

---

* Black did have a nervous breakdown, and on July 19, 1930, he shot himself in the head at his country estate near Huntington, Long Island.
† Altemus handwrote the name "Enry Hay Hick" over the actual name "Henry Clay Frick," also changing his daughter's name from "Helen" to "Ellen" and writing "Hick" over "Frick" elsewhere in the manuscript.
‡ Helen Clay Frick (1888-1984) was the daughter of Adelaide Howard Childs and Henry Clay Frick, the industrialist, financier, and art patron, who was chairman of the Carnegie Steel Company and helped facilitate the creation of the U.S. Steel Corporation.

because of her unanswered communications to her brother's many appeals for assistance.

My letter to Miss Hick told of her mother's request from Palm Beach, a few years before, to visit treasured Eden, and Beau's permission and invitation granted because of my great admiration for her uncle, a grand old man. I told her of my loneliness for Tidbits and my hope of bringing him to New York and that any courtesy she might tender would be greatly appreciated.

A few days later I received a short note from her secretary saying only, that New York City had agencies to handle these problems.

STRUBER & COMPANY

With Miss Hick's munificent advice in mind, I called again at the College Bureau and found a cordial reception awaiting me.* The busy banking house of Struber & Company was looking for a college graduate to act as private secretary to its President, who was leaving shortly for a cruise of the Mediterranean. The young lady fortunate enough to secure this exalted secretaryship would work with the Vice-Presidents during Mr. Struber's sojourn abroad, thereby familiarizing herself with the Company's particular methods.†

The Bureau was confident the position was mine and equally positive of the splendid fee it would quickly grasp.

Five Vice-Presidents of this great organization interviewed me before I was notified of being the successful appicant. One of the five didn't approve as at a later time I saw his addendum to the Company's report as to my qualifications, which read,

---

* Many cities, including New York and Chicago, had College Bureaus that helped place teachers and others with some college training in professional fields like secretarial positions.
† Altemus handwrote the name "Struber" over the actual, but slightly misspelled, name "S. W. Strauss" in the title and wherever else it appeared in this chapter. Simon William Straus (1866-1930) was a prominent banker and philanthropist known as the founder of the mortgage real estate bond.

"Looks like a yokel"

The Vice-Presidents believed in long hours; the general offices seemed able to plan the days work so the stenographers and clerks could leave at five o'clock, but the executives were so busy holding meetings, watching the tickers nearby and attending luncheons that their secretaries rarely left before seven P.M.

The Bureau had informed me of the strict ban this Company had put on married women and bobbed heads but it didn't tell me of the great show I was to enjoy every morning about eight thirty, in the ladies dressing rooms.

At this time girl and young woman employees began to arrive, probably a hundred or more - switchboard operators, clerks, stenographers and secretaries. No one needed to report until nine but the half hour was necessary to array the ladies for the business day.

After discarding wraps, furs, galoshes and now and then a wedding ring and placing them in individual lockers, out of the same receptacles would appear wigs and transformations of all colors, black, brown, raven and auburn - understood the ban also covered blondes.

The girls would then arrange these costly tresses over their smart bobs and at nine o'clock were at their desks - not a bobbed head in the organization - but, those transformations were shifty and irritating and would necessitate frequent visits to the dressing rooms for adjustment of hairpins, nets. etc.

I decided the Company needed a systematizer as its valuable time was being wasted - one hour daily per capita, to adjust stray ringlets was entirely too much for the present age of time conservation.

Why "Big Bosses" demanded the long unsanitary tresses

of our grandmothers in this era of evolution was beyond my comprehension, as the ultra smart secretary of New York's Fifth Avenue would be most inconsistent when garbed in the chic business frock of the day to have a Physche knot on top of her head.*

However, thats the way heads of finance felt about the matter and stenographers and secretaries always acquiesce to the superior intelligence and integrity of their employers.

When the days work was over the girls would rush to their lockers, throw in the wigs and transformations, take out the wedding rings, and then carefully brush, amid utterances of comfort, their own lovely bobbed locks in preparation for the evening.

Everybody was selling bonds those days and making lots of money. Buildings were going up at rapid pace throughout the country and "never lost a dollar Struber" was financing huge projects everywhere. They were busy days and a competent secretary in this organization could talk to representatives in Pittsburgh, Philadelphia, St. Louis and Chicago on four different wires all at the same time.

My work apparently had been satisfactory and the future looked bright; my savings had accumulated sufficiently to send for Tidbits, place him in private school daytimes near Central Park, and lease for we two a charming little apartment.

Walking on Park Avenue one noonday I thought I recognized a familiar face - surely it must be, and yet the sylph-

---

* A Psyche knot was a common hairstyle in Edwardian England in which the hair is brushed back and twisted into a coil at the nape of the neck. Its name derives from the fact that the Greek goddess Psyche is often portrayed in paintings with this hairstyle.

like outline was not in a tailored suit - the entire ensemble too distinguished - the swing too graceful - she had always been hurried with no time for thought of harmonious motion - nevertheless I turned back and rushed after the charming resemblance.

"Babs" was all I could say, before she had grasped me in close embrace, crushing the orchid snuggling so securely amid lace concealed surfaces.

Babs   - "Why darling, can it really be
              you - oh I'm so happy to see you
              again - its ages and ages - where is
              Tidbits - where are you going - what
              are you doing in New York?"

Secretary   - "Oh, Babs dear, isn't this wonderful
              to meet again - how grand you look -
              thinner but gorgeous - have you a
              minute - can't we stop in somewhere
              and have a chat? I'm on my luncheon
              hour and must be back promptly at
              two."

Babs   - "You don't mean to tell me you are
              still sweeping cigarette stubs,
              sleuthing, and interviewing clients,
              do you?"

Secretary   - "Yes, I have a splendid position,
              good money, comfy little apartment,
              Tidbits is in school and we are very

happy. Can't you have dinner with
us tonight and we'll have a real old
memory test?"

Babs — "Sorry, old dear, right now I'm on
my way to luncheon at the Ritz;
after that a lesson in English and
etiquette; I'm really a student
now - seriously, am being trained
in the refinements of mind, morals
and taste. I'm in love, darling,
and you will remember I believe in
progression. Here's my loft" (handing
secretary visiting card) "phone me
the very first evening you can - love
to have you tonight - a few friends
dropping in late."

Secretary (noticing new name on card)

"Why, Babs - Barbara Doulane - the
Doulane - not married, dear?"

Babs — "Not now, lovely, but have been, no
tailors or doctors either - tell you
later."

With a kiss Babs whisked on and I returned to my duties of
interviews, typing, checking and long distance talking.

Nine o'clock that evening found me in Bab's penthouse apartment, a delightful place, restful and inviting through its sim-

plicity and good taste of furnishing and decoration. Babs had advanced towards true perfection, at least in so far as charm of home atmosphere might be concerned. She seemed so changed - the southern drawl so distinctive once was no longer negroid; she spoke with modulation and an English accent.

As she had been so chic in her neatly tailored suits, so now was she ultra smart in her daringly designed, but unadorned gown of cloudlike chiffon.

Babs   - "I'm expecting friends, dear; come
           on, lets get acquainted before
           interruptions; you can see yourself I
           have not had sleeping sickness since
           I lived at The Drake. Its been three
           years since you and Tidbits went to
           see the cows and haystacks - you
           never wrote and I decided my morals
           did not conform with your splendid
           ethics. You know, dear, your serene
           philosophy and my yielding theory
           of life's values do not coincide; it
           is beyond my comprehension why you
           still press those silly little a, b,
           and c's up and down, when you could
           have all this - beauty - money -
           companionship - Oh, darling, whats
           the use - have a cigarette?"

Secretary - "Thanks, how do you know I could, and
             besides there's Tidbits you know -
             He is really all I want, but if this

office ever discovers I'm not the
Miss they think I am it will be just
too bad again for me. Babs, dear, who
is writing the checks now - banker -
gangster - or is it still Doctor
Lerner?"

Babs -
(laughing)   "You won't believe me, will you? I
told you I had married again. Two
years ago I met a nice old dear at
The Drake - was a coal man from
Omaha - he had the gout and was
lonely - didn't like his relatives -
we married and spent two years
abroad - French boulevards - Italian
Riviera - North African Arabs - and
darling, those shieks of Algeria - by
the way, guess who Tubby introduced
me to in Paris?"

Secretary - "Beau?"

Babs   - "You said it, and did he ask for
you. He was being wheeled around
in a chair - I told him everything
about you, good, bad and indifferent,
and he asked me to tell you that
he was sorry you had deserted him.
As to Doctor Lerner guess he is
still playing poker and dissecting
the ladies. Husband Tubby suffered

terribly with his foot but refused
to obey the doctor's orders; he was
a lover of champagne and rich foods,
also other wild habits which were
positively forbidden him; well,
darling, he passed out suddenly one
morning a few months ago and the
lawyers advised me I was one of the
moneyed widows of Manhattan. Poor
Tubby, he lived high and died happy."

Secretary - "I never knew you were divorced, Babs."

- - - - - - - - - -

*A page, numbered 158-f, is missing
from the original manuscript. Althea
Altemus and Babs are joined by Babs's
friend Paul Durrance, and they are
being introduced.*

- - - - - - - - - -

Babs   - "Paul, gaze upon a confidential
weaver of big boss perplexities"

"and, you darling" tell me later what
you think of Paul Durrance, my majesty
supreme."

Paul   - "Charmed, I'm sure, wouldn't mind
at all daily business difficulties
with such a lovely aide. Really, now,

```
                    can't be the little mother secretary
                    Barbara told me she took to the poker
                    game?"

Secretary   -  "The same - do you know, Babs, that
                    was the only easy money I ever made,
                    thanks to you."
```

A few intelligentsia joined our trio, and Babs held her own during discussions of dramatis personae, the dual alliance, the triple entente, abject morals, archaism and prohibition. Babs was advancing mentally at rapid pace.

It was late - Babs mint juleps were producing pleasant quiverings - someone was strumming Bartlett's Dream on a guitar and sweet drowsiness was welcoming - then, a sudden awakening as Babs laughingly whispered:

```
Babs        -  "Darling, I want you to meet a dear
                    friend of ours, a charming chap, Mr.
                    Larry Norton, business man - my true
                    friend Mrs. _____"

(Secretary quickly arising - recognizing one of
her "Big Boss" Vice-Presidents)

Secretary   -  "Delighted, Mr. Norton."

Mr. Norton -
(grinning)     "Well, this is a surprise Mrs.
                    _____ a pleasure, indeed, to find
                    such a jewel in its proper setting."
```

Secretary   - "Precious gems, Mr. Norton, require
                no mountings to enhance their worth.
                I guess you refer to a diamond in the
                rough, do you not?"

Mr. Norton - "Why, of course not, why do you think
                I'm jesting; really I mean it."

Secretary   - "Have you forgotten your memo. on
                that august application blank of
                mine."

Mr. Norton - "Really, I don't recall; please tell
                me, what did I say."

Secretary
(Turning away)-"Looks like a yokel."

Calling Babs aside I advised her of this latest calamity but she told me not to worry; she said that although Mr. Norton might have passed a remark intimating a person looked like a yokel nevertheless he would be the last man in the world to discharge a secretary because she had a Tidbits; confidentially she informed me that Mr. Norton's infidelities were numerous - that he was always fearful his business associates would discover his immoral life - he had married money and cautiously guarded his clandestine love-affairs - she and Paul would pledge him to secrecy.

Tidbits and I were awfully happy for sometime and then our Jonah really cropped up once more.

The Superintendent of our apartment house, in casual conversation one day, advised that an investigator from Struber &

Company asked him about a thousand questions as to just what sort of person I was - whether or not I kept late hours, did I pay my bills, did I live with my parents, was I an addict of drugs, did I imbibe in intoxicating beverages or did I have any other bad habits. The interrogator informed the superintendent that he was not seeking information because I was under any sort of suspicion but that I was an employee of a great organization who prided itself on its intricate investigation bureau and modern systems.

The Superindent told the questioning person that he was wasting his time, that I was one of the best tenants they had; that my evenings were spent helping my son to get his lessons, etc. etc.

I knew then that the reports of my private life would soon be on the desk of my chief. He was a peach of a fellow but I had told him I was a Miss and although my work had been satisfactory I didn't feel like facing the deception.

Whatever crime it is for a woman, who has been left a widow, to wish to earn her own living and keep her child with her, I do not know - but crime it seems to be.

To the big business man children should be placed in an orphanage or institution - at least out of the life of a private secretary.

I resigned from this noble organization the following day, feigning sudden, serious illness, rather than face the music that I had an adorable son.

* *

(SKETCH THIRTEEN)

SKETCH 13

PIGEONBLOOD RUBY

As private secretary to a diamond merchant my future reflected much light.

TOSH, my chief, was as brilliant as the gems he so generously displayed. Not good looking but substantial in proportion, rotund, sleek, jovial and slightly inebriated, he commanded attention wherever he went.

Tosh had worked very hard when a boy and his education had been sadly neglected; he had been an office boy in a jewelry house and what schooling he had was picked up in night schools whenever the purse strings would permit. From office boy to clerk, salesman and Amsterdam buyer had taken twenty years, during which time Tosh saved every penny he could spare for the nest egg which would start him in business some day. He was now fifty-five and in the many years he had been in business for himself wealth and success had gradually pyramided until he now enjoyed a town apartment as well as a great estate in Westchester hills.*

Tosh was a commuter - that is when he visited the family -

---

* It is not clear who "Tosh" is, though the description bears a degree of resemblance to Harry Winston, one of the leading purveyors of diamonds and rare gems in the world. Many of the details do not accord, however.

TOSH

and to see that he left the office in Maiden Lane in time to catch the 5:15 at Grand Central Station was no simple task.* Mrs. Tosh would usually phone at 3:30 and ask if Mr. Tosh expected to join the family at dinner. During the first weeks in his office the question would be relayed but found it was annoying as he would bluntly remark "Of course I <u>expect</u> to." Later on my observation became keen and I could inform Mrs. Tosh adeptly whether or not he would be one of the diners. Invariably a luncheon with one of his many blonde enchantresses would necessitate frequent helpings from the decanter in the upper drawer of his personal file. Tosh would then doze at intervals and the switchboard operator would be advised that Mr. Tosh was in conference and must not be disturbed. When roused he would become very much occupied with documents of importance, but before five o'clock he would request that I phone his Japanese butler in the town apartment to prepare dinner for two. Days when Tosh lunched alone he didn't nap in the afternoons; at such times I informed Mrs. Tosh that her husband would make the 5:15.

Tosh told me he had never needed a private secretary until now; said all his time had been given to business and didn't have time for a secretary; but now, that he had more leisure for joy of living he really needed a clever girl to keep his appointments straight and use discretion in telephone messages. All his calls from now on would be immediately switched to my wire; he said many ladies would phone relative to purchases of jewelry - and other matters of importance - and he would trust to my good judgment to treat all matters in strictest of confidence. He said he was worried at the moment over some threatening letters

* Maiden Lane was the center of the jewelry trade in New York until the late 1920s and early 1930s.

he had received; they were from a woman he tried to befriend but she was ungrateful and felt he should finance an European trip or make a settlement of some kind. She was a Gladys Miller and any phone messages or calls from the lady must be handled with diplomacy. He didn't wish the matter to go to the attention of Mrs. Tosh, or the courts, and any compromise I might negotiate with Miss Miller would be more than appreciated.

Tosh's business was not confined to New York; he had stores in Chicago, Pittsburgh and St. Louis. Business in all cities was growing by leaps and bounds; women had lots of money to invest in diamonds and precious stones; in every city women would pay $1000.00 for a diamond paying one hundred per month, rather than five hundred dollars in cash. Tosh said women didn't have five hundred dollars all at one time but could easily obtain substantial amounts to make payments; that all accounts were confidential and husbands rarely knew the amounts their wives were investing in jewels. He said the poor men saps didn't know the value of stones and they believed their wives when advised that rare bargains had been picked up for small sums. Tosh would keep those ladies continuously on his books for when a purchase was almost paid a clever salesman would call on the lady with a companion piece - brooch - bracelet - dinner rings - only a few hundred which could be paid so much per month and hubby would never know. Very few of those companion pieces ever went back into stock.

Tosh informed me that he owned most of the stock in TOSH, INC. and although nearly all business was conducted through the corporation still he had a few friends and acquaintences to whom he, personally, sold on either cash or time payments, and those few accounts it would be necessary for me to take care of.

Tosh added that one of his best customers was a Mrs. Campbell, a much married lady who had several daughters; she was money mad in her youth and fond of travel; she was first married to an American and Greta, a lovely yellow haired girl was born. Later another daughter, Violet, became one of the family. Mr. Campbell died and while abroad an Italian became husband number two and Titania, now about twenty, was the offspring of that union. The Italian had not been a good provider and after a divorce Mrs. Campbell had married a Turk, Pasha Kahn, and Carmelita was the issue of that indiscretion. Tosh said that Pasha Kahn didn't like America and the then Mrs. Kahn didn't care for Turkey, so she, accompanied by the four daughters, returned to New York and were living in luxurious quarters in the East Sixties. The mother used her first husband's name of Campbell and lived in seclusion with her attractive daughters and their friends. They loved jewels and Mrs. Campbell or one of the girls phoned frequently for Tosh to call with uncut diamonds, rubies, sapphires, mountings or other unique pieces of jewelry. He told me they were his best personal customers and he made one-hundred percent profit on all he sold them above the TOSH, INC. listed prices. The family netted him about ten thousand per year and every little bit helped.

When asked why the Campbells never came to the store to make purchases Mr. Tosh replied that the girls were so beautiful that they were never permitted out of the house.

One afternoon Tosh was having longer naps than usual when a call came on the phone from Mrs. Campbell.

When informed that Mr. Tosh was out she petulantly remarked, "Do you suppose he will be in soon. It is Titania's birthday and she wants a pigeonblood ruby - ring or earrings of good size. Tell Mr. Tosh to bring out something this afternoon sure," and the bang in the receiver told me she didn't expect an answer.*

Tosh awakened sufficiently to ask who was on the wire and when told of the conversation he asked for a bromo seltzer. Draining the glass he drawled, "there's one thousand dollars faded because that luncheon dizzy daughter insisted on champagne - hic - now don't think I'm intoxicated - I'm not - hic - I can't go out there - fellows waiting to hold me up - no, not steady enough - hic - too bad, damn that fat Albino - hic."

Begging Tosh to let me go in his place and allow me a ten percent commission didn't succeed at first; he only took another whisky, rocked back and forth in his swivel chair and laughed, as he said, "No, that wouldn't do a tall - not a tall."

"Oh, Mr. Tosh, please, that ten percent commission would help so much - am sure I would come back with a big order - its her birthday and if we don't deliver something in an hour Tiffany or Blackstone & Frost will make the sale. Please let me go, Mr. Tosh."

He just continued to stare and laugh and then blurted out, "Hum, I believe you could - you see

* Rubies the color of pigeon's blood were considered the finest rubies because their hue was the deepest and they were said to be the purest. They most often came from Mogok, a region in northern Burma (now Myanmar).

```
women don't go there - hic - its early afternoon -
well, maybe - all over five hundred on the ruby
you get."
```

Wondering why women were not accepted at Mrs. Campbells it seemed advisable not to intrude, but after Tosh instructed me to get his personal box from the safe and marveling at the jewels he took therefrom I decided to take a chance.

```
"Titania", said Tosh, "needs these ruby
earrings - hum - she has the ring, bracelet and
brooch - hic - I want five hundred - pigeonblood -
ha ha."
```

Tosh placed the earrings together with a string of pearls and lapis ring in a tissue paper package and then the paper packet into a leather wallet which securely clasped. He asked me to place the wallet in my blouse and see that it was secure; after another whisky straight requested that I get Mrs. Campbell on the phone saying he wanted to talk to her.

What she said I do not know but Tosh's remarks ran something like this;

```
"Hello, Molly, this you? Un Huh - say Molly
I'm sick - so sick I can't move - - - - got the
grippe - - - hic - - I'm sending my secretary with
a big bargain - - - - sure its all right - - -
watch for her - - - taxi - navy blue suit, slight,
young, hic, pretty - - - un huh - - - of course
not, green as grass - - - strictly business - -
well, they're your daughters aren't they - un huh."
```

Arriving in the East Sixties the taxi stopped at a three story brown stone front, the last one in the block. It was an old home and I was elated at the anticipation of meeting Mrs. Campbell and her lovely daughters.

The door opened before there was time to ring and a colored maid ushered me into a spacious sanctum. Brilliant embroidered satin hangings of orange, cerise and yellow adorned the walls harmonizing with the deep, soft Turkish rugs; low divans with cushions and pillows of all the colors of the rainbow challenged the oriental lanterns reflecting a million titanic diamonds from the mirrored ceiling. Teak wood taborettes and a Turkish water pipe completed the furnishings with the exception of the marble likeness of Physche at the Well. The room was one of contrast, beauty and mystery.

The maid said Madam would be down in a minute. She was in error; it was sometime before glamorous Mrs. Campbell put in an appearance - a stately creature - a whispering echo of a beauty salon.

Mrs. Campbell said the girls were at breakfast (it was almost three P.M.) but if I would display the jewels on the taborette Titania would select what she wanted. The rubies were sparkling and radiating all the colors of the lanterns above as Titania noiselessly entered the room.

Titania did not acknowledge the introduction; she seemed unaware of my presence but eagerly picked up the earrings with an expression of awe. Could it be possible that such a beautiful creature might be deaf and dumb - reminded one of Nita, an Iris - like wine that quickens the senses and brightens the eyes. Titania's flimsy drapery and carmine sandals were set off by anklets, bracelets and rings of rubies and diamonds. She turned, smiled and brokenly said:

```
"Like em - give you now hundred dollar - how
much they cost?"
```

Telling her they were six hundred dollars and asking how she wished to pay the balance, she added,

```
"Das all right, Mr. Tosh, he arrange."
```

It was apparent that Titania did not speak much English. She nonchalantly clasped the earrings under the dark curly bob and smiled as three flushed and laughing girls entered the room together. They, too, were in negligee of one type or another and all three were whiffing at gold tipped cigarettes.

They were a strange assembly, a combination of passion and peace - sparkling eyed beauties in their rainbow ensembles - young laughter - exotic flowers - calm, serene and unruffled as is all perfection. I was fascinated - such an unusual family - not a trace of resemblance between mother or daughters - an unforgettable visit as are only a few of our human memories.

A maid softly told Titania that a friend was waiting and she quickly and quietly left the room. Thinking my work was completed I was jubilant when Carmelita said she would take the lapis and Violet the string of pearls. They both gave me the required deposit in brand new bills and Violet offered me fifty dollars for my navy blue suit saying she never owned a suit.*

Telling Mrs. Campbell not to bother about phoning for a taxi and hastening through the vestibule I almost knocked down a young man in a tweed suit descending the stairs. He, too, was in a hurry, but unfortunately only one taxi was waiting at the curb.

```
* Altemus's description of Mrs. Campbell's "home" clearly suggests
that it was a brothel.
```

"I'll be glad to have you share my taxi – no
other in sight", said the young man.

"Am going down town, guess another will be
along in a minute, thanks just the same", I
remarked appreciatively.

"Going to 34th and Fifth – come on – take you
that far anyway" added this pleasant fellow.

Getting into the taxi the following conversation took
place;

Young Man   – "Well, well, its three o'clock – fine
time to be getting to my office.
How's business with you these days?"

Secretary   – "Splendid, thanks, made over two
hundred today."

Young man, (turning quickly to look at secretary)
"Hum – not bad – you look fresh as
a new dollar bill too – what's your
name, don't recall seeing you around
Campbell's before?"

Secretary   – "Are you Mrs. Campbell's son?

Young Man   – "Am I what – yee Gods – say bright
eyes whats the big idea – are you

kidding me or am I still asleep - who are you anyway."

Secretary - "I'm a private secretary from Maiden Lane."

Young man - "Well I be dammed - thats a new one - you're all right kiddo - how about a little date tomorrow - shall I ask for Pansy, Magnolia, Daisy or Rose?"

Secretary - "No thanks, you see I don't make dates - I have a little boy at home who appreciates me more."

Young man - "Oh, yeah?"

Secretary - "Yeah".

Young man - "Will you please tell me what you were doing out at Molly's?"

Secretary - "Don't know any Molly. I told you I'm a secretary to a diamond broker in Maiden Lane. Mrs. Campbell's daughter, Titania, has a birthday today and she wanted a pigeon blood ruby - not only sold her earrings but made a plenty on lapis and pearls sold to her sisters."

Young man - "Well, I'll be dammed."

Secretary   -   "Here's where I leave you - thanks a
                 lot."

Young man   -   "Say, sister, seriously, take my
                 advice; when Titania or Carmelita
                 want any more jewels send your boy
                 friend with the gems - that'll make
                 it profitable and sensible for all
                 concerned."

Leaving the taxi, another took me quickly to the office. Tosh apparently had helped himself generously to the decanter as he was sound asleep. Phoning his Japanese servant he arrived in time to help Tosh to his apartment to keep the appointment for dinner.

The next day Tosh complimented me on my success as a saleswoman but added that selling was like betting on the races - the smart person who won on a first bet usually quit before getting stung.

Months went by quickly and happily at this work although Tosh drank more and more. Miss Miller furnished him with plenty to think about but in due time she left on her European trip well supplied with cash.

One morning Tosh told me the doctors said he must go away for awhile to take treatments for his liver, but Mrs. Tosh informed me that he was going to have the Keeley cure and would not be back at the office for sometime. She suggested that I look for another position inasmuch as the doctor insisted that Tosh retire from active work.*

* The Keeley Cure was a controversial treatment for alcoholism developed by Leslie Keeley in Dwight, Illinois, in 1879.

The last day at the office before leaving for the sanitorium Tosh imbibed freely - to say the least - but before he became entirely intoxicated I asked him if Mrs. Campbell were really the mother of Greta, Violet, Titania and Carmelita. He laughed and replied "That's her tale and she cleaves thereto."

JOHN J. SINCH & CO.

John J. Sinch, New York builder, was the next big boss needing a secretary. He had a perfectly good one, who had taken care
of his business for many years, but like all other nouveau riche a
complete new scheme for everything must be arranged.*

He had been living with his family on Central Park West but
recently moved to Fifth Avenue. His new offices on Madison
Avenue were distinguished for spaciousness, regal furnishing
and decoration.

Noticing an unusual advertisement in the New York Times
for a private secretary I answered the same and in about a week
was requested to call for interview. Two gentlemen talked with
me, one I pleasantly remember as the architect for the Company.† He was cultured, quiet and unassuming and I am confident that the success I had in landing this secretaryship was

---

* Altemus handwrote the name "John J. Sinch" over the actual name
"Fred F. French" in the title and wherever else it appeared in this
chapter. Frederick Fillmore French (1883-1936) was a real estate developer and builder in New York. Altemus provided the correct streets
for French's residence and business.
† The architect for Fred F. French was H. Douglas Ives, who designed
the "Mesopotamian" features of the Fred French Building, including
the colored terra-cotta panels, sunburst designs, and Assyrian-style
griffins.

due to the recommendations of this delightful chap - he told me that out of hundreds of applicants I was best qualified for the work.

First impressions are lasting ones;

The introduction to Mr. Sinch may have been as disappointing to him as to me. In the first place he had called me on the phone and asked that I meet him at his office at five P.M. - I waited outside of his rooms until seven o'clock before we talked.

He told me the position was mine and that anyone connected with his organization would have great opportunities for wealth; that he expected to be a power in New York some day. He said his people were poor, and when a boy he had been a timekeeper on building projects; that his superiors had been severe with him but that now he was approaching the top of the ladder and it amused him to bring into his organization his former bosses, and dictate to them as they had dictated to him years before.

This secretaryship was not pleasing to me and one day I left for luncheon and failed to return.

* *

MIAMI

Guess you know the old story about "Once you get Florida sands in your shoes" - well, its true.

It was 1925 and everyone in New York was talking of people becoming rich over night in Miami - some kind of real estate boom. Tidbits and I had some money and who knew the charm of that city better than we; Miami, where it's always June; Chicago and New York experiences had not been over lucrative - too much competition - too many long hours getting to and from wherever one wanted to go - expensive living and miserable weather - well, we would go back to God's country and see how such sudden wealth was acquired.

We didn't recognize old Miami on arrival; instead of the lovely long avenues of royal, coconut and Washingtonian palms, the funny parasol fringed Victorias driven by colored boys with Panama hats, red and green bicycles, and lazy maidens with mantillas and duennas, we found new boulevards with New York skylines; Rolls Royces, Cadillacs, Packards and Pierce Arrows parked on every available space; and a regular Fifth Avenue crowd on Twelfth Street; it just wasn't the old place at all, a Metropolis had been erected.

We opened the green and white cottage, repaired and refurnished same; we found old Mammy who was happy to be back with us after the years of separation; and I found secretaryship to a New York real estate wizard who had drifted south a few months before.*

Many stories have been written of the Florida boom and most everyone knows, how millions upon millions of dollars were invested in Miami with which to build three mile bridges, sky-scraper hotel and office buildings, apartments and great private estates; of islands being made in Biscayne Bay due to the insufficient available land for sale; of Miami's enchanting sister, Coral Gables, the beauty spot of America, due to its adamant policy of all building and landscaping being supervised by its eminent Architect; and of the great estates designed at Miami Beach for the sophisticates of the world. The city had a half million residents whereas three years before there were but twenty thousand.

(SKETCH FOURTEEN)

Bands were playing in most offices day and night; these were for the amusement of northerners who were pouring into town with their years of savings to buy land and share in this gigantic gold brick. The city was gay and everyone was happy playing the game of getting something for nothing.

How my big bosses here have kept out of Atlanta I don't know; we would buy acreage and pay the first payment; then we would divide the acreage into lots and next day sell all the lots accepting as initial payment on each one the amount of our down payment on the total amount of land; we didn't bother about the balance due on the property for that would take care of itself later when the lot purchasers completed their payments;

* Altemus moved back to Miami in 1925 and began work as a stenog-rapher for the Barnaby Agency, a real estate firm based in New York and founded by Frank A. Barnaby in 1924.

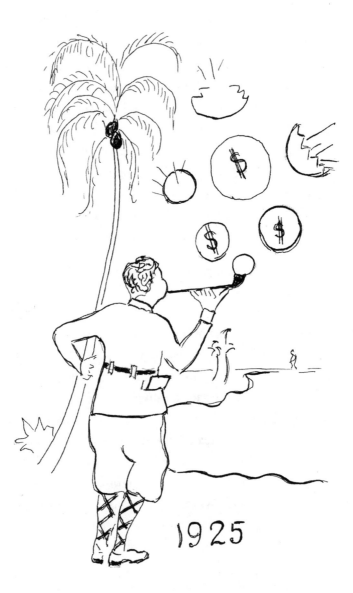

1925

SKETCH 14

but, some of those buyers paid all cash for their pieces of land and received deeds for property that was not released from the original mortgage.

No one, bosses, sellers or buyers had time to waste thinking of releases, abstracts or other foolish papers; all anyone asked was some sort of receipt showing deposit on a certain piece of land so the signed paper could be sold next day to some other sucker.

In the latter part of 1925 we were all millionaires - on paper at least. Tidbits and I added a country place, an island retreat and an Ashville log cabin to our list of abodes; we needed more automobiles and our scale of living increased by leaps and bounds.

It was grand to experience wealth, all our own, if only for a short time.

One night in 1926, from out of a clear sky, came a wind, speeding along at one hundred and fifty miles an hour, and blew away two of our abodes, and then three years later, 1929, something went wrong in the stock market up in New York, for it swept away the rest of our riches invested in what we thought were golden securities.*

However, joyousness invades Miami today; the real estate inflation and the hurricane are forgotten; the city is unique with its present business activity, and its charming home atmosphere where one senses a change in the pulse-beat of life through true beauty and serious living.

(SKETCH FIFTEEN)

---

* The hurricane of 1926 was one of the deadliest and costliest in American history. Over three hundred people died and property losses were estimated to be over $75 million in 1926 dollars. The destruction brought an abrupt halt to the land boom of the 1920s, and, as a result, Miami experienced economic recession before it hit the nation overall after the 1929 stock market crash.

TID·BITS – NOW

SKETCH 15

BISCAYNE BAY

Last night was Good Friday and amid a dozen or so of Hot Cross Buns, I had the pleasure of listening to the adventures of "THE REAL McCOY", whose stories were published not so long ago in LIBERTY MAGAZINE. With him were his brother, Ben, and his secretary, Helen, and what an interesting trio they are.*

We were on their cruising houseboat, "CORAL REEF", anchored in the placid shimmering waters of Biscayne Bay.

What a picture from the stern - the dying Miami day painting the tiles of the city with farewell splendor in tints of orange, red and apricot, and the blue tropic night swiftly descending on the lovliest land that human eyes have ever seen; Tidbits and his friends tying up their sailboat after a happy day on the keys; yachts of the Vanderbilts, Mellons, Cyrus Curtis and the Astors close by; and a wandering troubador with his guitar seranading with rich repertoire of melodies the ROMANCE from New York.

The perfume of night blooming jasmine, the strumming of palm fronds and now and then a lovely strain of Beethoven's Moonlight Sonata wafting in from LaMonica's Concert Band under the aura of colored lights in the park fascinated all; we

* Altemus is referring to William Frederick "Bill" McCoy (1877-1948), the sea captain, boat builder, and notorious rum-runner during Prohibition.

were under the spell of Miami's langourous beauty and told our stories of adventure.*

Bill told how when they were in India one of the very great Maharaghas, who had entertained them at dinner, so fancied Helen that he offered to trade five of his most beautiful wives for her; who could blame him for what a dear she really is.

You see, Bill, Ben and Helen have traversed the seven seas for several years and have gathered treasures from all over the world; lanterns from Africa, swords from Roumania, teakwood and jade from China, but most to my fancy was the tiny piano with its deep dulcet tone, which gave me an hour's happiness paying the old fashioned melodies of my childhood - trust my host was not bored with my interpretation.

In conclusion let me say, that were I twenty again, nothing would be sweeter than a private secretaryship such as Helen's; just to drift hither and yon, writing and painting, sailing from port to port, and letting the world go by.

THE END

Mrs. Althea Altemus
63 S.E. 6th St
Miami Fla

* Caesar LaMonaca (1896-1980) was the Italian-born conductor of Miami's symphonic band that played free outdoor concerts at the Bayfront Park Band Shell.

AFTERWORD: CHRONICLING THE CLERICAL LIFE OF ALTHEA ALTEMUS

Robin F. Bachin

Althea Altemus's "Big Bosses" is a lively account of the daily lives of celebrities and politicians, industry titans, and working women in Jazz Age America. In fact, the manuscript is many different genres in one. It is a detective story, with disguised names that demand that the reader hunt for clues to uncover the true identities of the subjects she presents. It is an exposé of the lives of some of the most prominent businessmen in the 1920s, as Altemus provides firsthand accounts of their comings and goings, daily routines, personal foibles, and, of course, their romantic lives. And it is a memoir that provides rare insight into the life of a single working mother in the first decades of the twentieth century. Althea describes the lunches, poker games, house parties, and theatrical performances she attended with various female friends, showcasing the increasing freedom and independence that wage-earning women experienced by the 1920s. Yet Altemus also details the elaborate lengths she went to in order to hide the fact that she had a child. She highlights the dangers that often accompanied the need to make a living in a society that still shunned single mothers.[1]

Altemus begins "Big Bosses" with her employment at Vizcaya, the luxurious Miami winter residence of American businessman James Deering that was constructed on the shores of

Biscayne Bay as an elaborate Italianate villa. Over the years, Vizcaya's architecture, interiors, and gardens have been published extensively. Yet because the bulk of material left behind by Deering and his heirs concerns either the details of Vizcaya's construction or corporate records related to the family business, International Harvester, we know little about his life at Vizcaya.

Altemus's memoir fills in many of those details and adds many more. Altemus recounts with eloquence and wit the variety of experiences she had working for Deering. As Deering's private secretary at Vizcaya, Althea had access to Deering's daily life, correspondence, and issues and concerns in a way that few others did. She tells humorous and engaging stories about how Deering smuggled liquor into Vizcaya during Prohibition, how wealthy male guests cavorted with mistresses at Vizcaya while their wives went off to sleep in one of the many elegant guest rooms, and how female celebrities attempted to curry favor with Deering through surprise visits and gifts. The manuscript provides a behind-the-scenes peek into daily life at one of America's grandest Jazz Age homes and the guests who frequented it.

Altemus subtitles the preface to "Big Bosses" as "A Story of Actual Happenings," and she asserts that the content is factual with the exception of names. Research at Vizcaya and elsewhere substantiates the veracity of her assertion, demonstrating that, while some elements of the narrative have been fabricated, countless details in "Big Bosses" correspond with and expand upon archival references. Moreover, despite the tell-all qualities of her account, Altemus also is careful to recount stories that are sensitive to the cast of characters she encountered.

Decades after writing "Big Bosses," Altemus demonstrated her interest in veracity by writing notes in the margins of an article in the *American Weekly* detailing which aspects of the story describing Vizcaya's official opening on Christmas 1916 were true and which were embellishments (the servants dressed in gold-faced uniforms) or outright falsehoods (the story that the entire cast of the Ziegfeld Follies performed at a pretentious party hosted at Vizcaya, and the notion that Deering had suffered a "secret sorrow"). On top of a drawing accompanying the article of two beautiful women peering down on Vizcaya, presumably suggesting that Deering was a ladies' man, Altemus wrote, "What's this; no."[2]

Beyond her experiences at Vizcaya, Altemus's memoir describes in rich detail the lives of many other "big bosses" and her time working for them. The number of business leaders and celebrities for whom she worked or with whom she had encounters is extraordinary. In addition to Deering, she worked for Samuel Insull, president of Chicago Edison; New York banker and philanthropist S. W. Straus; prominent real estate developer Fred F. French; and possibly Harry S. Black, New York developer, contractor, and social club organizer. In the course of her travels and employment, Altemus met actresses Marion Davies, Constance Talmadge, and Jetta Goudal; aviator Glenn Curtiss; orator, presidential candidate, and secretary of state William Jennings Bryan; artist John Singer Sargent; inventor Thomas Edison; art patron Helen Clay Frick, the daughter of Carnegie Steel chairman Henry Clay Frick; and Phineas Paist, the artist and architect who played a central role in the building of Vizcaya as well as the planned suburb of Coral Gables, Florida (and who provided the original illustrations for Altemus's memoir).

"Big Bosses" addresses many elements of economic, social, and cultural life in Jazz Age America from the perspective of a single working mother. Altemus portrays the disruptions taking place in 1920s America from a very personal vantage point—one that is as compelling as the lives of the rich and famous. In this chronicle of her life as a working woman from a small factory town who makes her way in the world as a single mother, negotiating workplace discrimination and housing challenges, she poignantly portrays her hardships but also reveals her pluck, determination, humor, and adventurous spirit. Her captivating tale gives readers a deeper appreciation for the complexities of women's lives in Jazz Age America.

* * *

Althea Altemus was born as Althea Maggie McDowell on December 4, 1885, in Woodstock, Illinois, where her Scottish-American parents, Charles and Emma Pierce McDowell, lived. Woodstock was a small farming village and the seat of McHenry County. In the early twentieth century, Woodstock became known as "typewriter city" because both the Emerson and Oliver Typewriter Companies were located there.[3] Althea's parents had lived previously in Elgin, where Charles had grown up and where his parents continued to live. Elgin, located about thirty-five miles west of Chicago along the Fox River, grew in the 1840s and 1850s after the construction of the Galena and Chicago Union Railroad. The town is best known for the Elgin National Watch Company, which opened in 1866 and employed close to three thousand people by 1904. Both of Althea's parents had worked at the watch factory prior to moving to Woodstock, with Charles working in the dial department and Emma working as a jewel polisher. Their first child, Clarence, was born in Elgin in 1884 when Emma and Charles lived in one of the many worker's cottages near the factory. It is unclear why they moved to Woodstock, but fairly soon after Althea's birth, the family moved back to Elgin, where Charles resumed his employment in the dial department and became active in company sporting activities.[4]

Althea's family moved several times during her early childhood, living in various row houses and cottages near the Elgin watch factory, on Villa Street, Center Street, and then Raymond Street. Both Althea and Clarence attended school in Elgin, most likely finishing their studies at the public high school. There is no record of Althea graduating, though she is listed in the Elgin City Directory as a high school student in 1903, when she was eighteen years old. While at Elgin High School, she would have had the opportunity to take classes in commerce, bookkeeping, and stenography, which would have prepared her for her future work as a secretary. In 1905, Althea moved out of her parents' house at 334 Raymond Street, which her father purchased the same year, and appears to have taken a room just up the street as a boarder at 275 Raymond Street. This is the year she began commuting to a job as a stenographer in the famous Monadnock Building, at 53 West Jackson in downtown Chicago.[5]

Althea entered the workforce in a period when clerical labor was being both mechanized and feminized. As historians have shown, the nature of clerking was changing. While the job of clerk had previously been held by men and seen as a stepping-stone to advancement, it was increasingly held by women and downgraded in both creativity and status; there was little opportunity for career growth.[6] Clerks now had specialized, routine tasks, and they were closely overseen by managers. In 1870 women made up less than 3 percent of clerical workers, but by 1920 they were 49 percent of them. Copyists, clerks who handwrote in neat and legible form rough drafts of various office documents and letters, were replaced by female typists and stenographers, while the introduction of the telephone brought more women as mechanical operators, replacing skilled male telegraphers. This led to greater rationalization of the office, and more diversified job titles, with men having greater access to supervisory positions than women.[7]

There were a variety of reasons why women entered the clerical workforce in large numbers at the turn of the century. Many saw clerical labor as a respectable alternative to factory work or farm labor. The hours for clerical workers were shorter, work conditions better and cleaner, positions more secure, white-collar labor more prestigious, and pay better than in other positions open to women.[8] Middle-class women, many of whom could not afford the college education necessary to pursue traditionally female professions like teaching, social work, or library science, looked to clerical work as an occupation in which they could be trained quickly and inexpensively. By 1900, one-fifth of America's 25 million women were in the workforce, but only some had the opportunity to enter the clerical workforce.[9] To be considered for clerical work, women had to be literate in English, and most white employers only hired white, native-born women.

Clerical labor was a good option for Althea, then, if she wanted to avoid the difficult conditions of production work in the watch factory and earn higher wages, become more independent, and create a more secure future for herself. The long commute from Elgin as well as her ability to earn higher wages in Chicago most likely led to her decision to move into the city in 1908, where she lived in the Uptown neighborhood. She had changed jobs and was working as a secretary on Van Buren Street downtown when tragedy struck her family. In October of 1909, her brother, Clarence, who had been working at the watch factory in Elgin, drowned in the St. Joseph River in South Bend,

Indiana. The river was a popular place for outdoor recreation but apparently also had a treacherous grade, and over the years several people lost their lives by falling into the river and getting swept up in the current.[10]

Althea continued living in Chicago following the tragedy, and it was here that she met her future husband, Wayne Hughes Altemus; they married just four months after her brother's death. Wayne Altemus came from a prosperous family in Philadelphia who traced their lineage back to Germany, where Johann Friederich Althomus was born in 1716. Johann, Wayne Altemus's great-great grandfather, immigrated to the United States in 1740 along with his brother and purchased land in Cheltenham Township, just north of Philadelphia. Subsequent generations moved to Philadelphia and opened dry goods businesses, worked in automotive parts manufacturing, as book publishers, and as jewelry merchants. Wayne's grandfather, Samuel Taylor Altemus, is listed as a "Gentleman" in the 1850 census, with real estate holdings valued at $100,000. Samuel's son, Edward John, was a dry goods merchant. He married Medorah Levy, eldest daughter of John Patterson Levy and Mary Ann Levy (Owens), and by the 1880 census they had six children, including Wayne, born November 30, 1874. The family was prosperous: in 1880 it had five servants, including a cook, a laundress, a waitress, and a nurse.[11]

Wayne Altemus worked as a bookbinder in Philadelphia from 1900 until 1905, when he moved to Chicago to work as a clerk at S. T. Altemus & Co., diamond merchants and gold- and silversmiths. Wayne's brother Samuel presumably started the Philadelphia-based company and expanded it to Chicago. Just prior to Wayne's marriage to Althea, he was living on the Near South Side, at 1550 Prairie Avenue, while she was living several blocks south at 2926 South Lake Park Avenue, where she had moved in 1909. He was commuting downtown, as was she, so perhaps they met on the train ride to work. However the couple met, they married in Milwaukee on February 5, 1910. They remained in Chicago at least through the spring of that year, but by November of 1910 they had moved to Philadelphia, where they stayed until 1913.[12]

There is little information about Wayne and Althea during their first years in Philadelphia; they do not appear in the city directory. They likely lived with Wayne's mother, who by that time was widowed and living at 124 South Fortieth Street, near the University of Pennsylvania. Wayne's uncle, Lyman Beecher Childs, lived with them as well—a connection Althea would use in 1923, when she sought advice from Childs's half sister, Helen Clay Frick. Sometime in 1912, Wayne and Althea moved to Narberth, a Main Line suburb of Philadelphia. On August 14, 1912, their first son, Wayne MacDowell Altemus, was born at the West Philadelphia Hospital for Women. He died after twelve hours, of atelectasis, or a collapsed lung. He was buried in the Altemus family vault at Woodlands Cemetery in Philadelphia.[13]

In January of 1913, Wayne and Althea moved to Elgin and lived in her parents' home. The trauma of her son's death may have prompted Althea's return to Illinois for the support of her family during this difficult time. Apparently Wayne had a hard time holding down work and started drinking excessively. The couple soon moved to Sheridan Road in Chicago, and Wayne began working as a jewelry salesman at S. T. Altemus & Co. once again. On August 6, 1913, Althea had another baby, Robert MacDowell Altemus, who is referred to as "Tidbits" in the "Big Bosses" manuscript. Althea's parents then put a down payment on a house for the couple in Evanston, but they lost the house

Photographic portrait of Robert Altemus ("Tidbits") as
a baby.

shortly after Wayne lost his job. By 1915, the couple was living in Chicago again with their son, but soon thereafter Wayne and Althea separated, and in 1916 Althea filed for divorce.

Wayne never responded to the summons in chancery. He appears to have moved back to Philadelphia, but the summons was returned. According to the bill of complaint, filed in October of 1916, Wayne had remained "in an intoxicated condition almost continually," and he was "wholly unfit to attend to his usual occupation and business." The complaint states that, in April of 1913, he was arrested on the charge of resisting an officer while intoxicated, and in 1914 he was dismissed from his job because of drunkenness. In March of 1915, he checked into the Grace Hospital in Detroit to receive treatment for his alcoholism, but by April of 1915 Wayne "resumed his drunken habits and remained continuously drunk" until May of 1915, at which point Althea left him, taking their son.[14]

Both Althea and her mother, Emma McDowell, had an opportunity to provide evidence in the divorce case. Althea claimed that Wayne was "drunk continuously from two months after I married him until the day I left him—a period of over five years." When asked if he had provided any financial support since she had left him, Althea stated that he sent five dollars once when her son needed an operation but nothing further. Althea's mother testified that "he was drunk all the time," and that he never paid any money toward the Evanston mortgage. The divorce decree, issued in May of 1917, stated that Wayne H. Altemus was guilty of habitual drunkenness and was "a person wholly unfit to have the care, custody, control, or education of his child." Althea was granted full custody of Robert, as well as the right to resume her maiden name of Althea McDowell. Despite this, under certain circumstances, such as her Miami City

Directory listings beginning in the late 1930s and the authorship of "Big Bosses," she retained the surname Altemus.

We have little evidence of what happened to Wayne following the divorce. His draft registration card of 1918 stated that he was working as a machinist at the Harlan Plant of Bethlehem Steel in Wilmington, Delaware, but he listed his permanent address as Angora Terrace in Philadelphia, where his mother and aunt also lived. There is no record of his whereabouts until August 24, 1922, when he died of an unspecified cause in Montclair, New Jersey. Wayne, like his infant son, was buried in the family mausoleum at Woodlands Cemetery in Philadelphia.[15]

Shortly after her divorce was official, Althea moved to Miami to accept the position with James Deering at Vizcaya. It is unclear how Altemus first met Deering, but it is likely that they met in Chicago, where he offered her the opportunity to become his personal secretary at his new South Florida home. A letter from Deering to his designer Paul Chalfin in November of 1917 mentions that he would like Louis Koons, Chalfin's partner, to come to Miami and "give my new private secretary and me information about the articles there."[16]

Althea's move to Miami in late 1917 or early 1918 no doubt offered the opportunity for a completely fresh start after the challenges she had faced. Miami then was a young frontier city, having only been incorporated in 1896. Recent arrivals from the north described Miami as a wild place, with overgrown mangroves, inadequate provisions for housing, and unbearable heat, humidity, and insects.[17] Despite these discomforts, Miami appealed to many for its tropical climate, lush foliage, and sand and surf. Indeed, real estate developers, landscape designers, and architects capitalized on this lure of the tropical landscape to create an urban oasis amid the balmy temperatures and clear waters that made South Florida a destination for travelers and permanent settlers alike by the late teens and early twenties. They touted the city's rapid growth, its new amenities, and its growing number of investors who sought to take advantage of the opportunities that could be found in the "Magic City."[18]

Developers Henry Flagler, Carl Fisher, and George Merrick took advantage of the newfound wealth generated by mergers and monopolies in industry and technology to create seaside resorts selling lifestyles of leisure to America's business titans. Businessmen like Cornelius Vanderbilt (railroads), Andrew Carnegie (steel), Andrew Mellon (banking), and James and Charles Deering (agricultural machinery) accrued enormous wealth in the days before antitrust legislation forced the breakup of such monopolies. Miami was emerging as the new winter playground of the rich, and already boasted golf courses, polo grounds, and yachting marinas by the time of World War I. Railroad construction and the accompanying hotel development meant that there were new opportunities for travel to Florida, and that the lures of South Florida's resorts could eventually entice wealthy northerners to buy land and build winter homes there.[19]

James Deering's Vizcaya estate along Miami's Biscayne Bay epitomized this quest to build lavish homes, seek rest and rejuvenation in the tropical landscape, and establish a haven for entertaining well-heeled guests. According to Vizcaya designer Paul Chalfin, the estate promised to be "a monument to the avowed dreams of pleasure and *bienetre* [well-being]."[20] Deering's 180-acre estate was modeled after European country houses, especially eighteenth-century Italian villas, with the design of the mansion and grounds adapted to the South Florida climate and topography. The house blended the finest decorative and architectural elements from Europe with contemporary

American craftsmanship and modern conveniences such as elevators, refrigerators, and an automatic telephone switchboard.[21]

Here Althea Altemus began her Miami journey, less than one year after the formal opening of the estate. Her work for Deering would be much different from the work she had been doing as a stenographer in Chicago. The estate and her employer had complex needs, leading to a diverse portfolio of responsibilities. She had daily access to Deering and was responsible for a wide range of tasks, from opening the mail, responding to letters, bookkeeping and accounting, handling salaries and payroll, and doing personal errands. Her work for Deering helped propel her career forward and gave her the opportunity to seek out more desirable and lucrative positions in the future. Indeed, Altemus was paid a salary that was commensurate with professional men on the estate. A report to Deering's accounts manager, William Lauderback, on January 13, 1920, lists employees who made over $1,000 in 1919. Altemus is included ($1,500) as well as the engineer ($1,205.75), the property manager ($1,516.66), and the superintendent ($1,249.98).[22] Clearly, she had transcended the mechanical, routine and low-compensated position of a typical clerk of the time.

Altemus's work spaces also were much more private and elaborate than those of a typical clerk. When she first arrived at Vizcaya, she used the Pantaloon Room as her office. The Venetian-inspired bedroom, finished in brightly colored paint and lacquer, had its own bathroom as well as a small foyer. By the spring of 1919, she occupied an office above the chauffeur's rooms, located across the street from the main house at the West Gate Lodge and designed by Phineas Paist. While not as extravagant as the Pantaloon Room, the new office still gave Altemus privacy atypical of most secretaries at that time.[23]

One of Althea's first responsibilities when she arrived at Vizcaya was to coordinate the employee subscriptions to U.S. Liberty Loan Bonds during World War I. All International Harvester employees were encouraged to participate, as were the employees at Vizcaya. Each month, Altemus tabulated the subscriptions, tracked down employees who did not fulfill their pledges, and reported the total amount raised. At one point, she reports that there will be more monthly subscribers as a result of a recent raise by Deering. "When these men were asked a week or so ago they did not feel that they could afford to subscribe but they have all received an increase in salary the past week and apparently changed their minds. They have agreed to pay $5.00 a month, beginning with the Nov. 1 payment." Five dollars per month was the typical contribution, and the one that Altemus routinely made as well.[24]

Miami offered Althea the opportunity to live in a house with her son, who was four years old when they moved there, and even eventually to purchase her own home. She first rented an apartment but soon she moved to a house at 715 Twentieth Street, where she had a boarder, Ruth Delainey, also a secretary from Chicago, to help with expenses and perhaps child care. Interestingly, in the 1920 census, she lists herself as widowed even though Wayne was still alive. In the 1920 Miami City Directory, she uses her maiden name of McDowell, but in 1921 she changed the spelling to MacDowell, perhaps to highlight her Scottish background lest the actual spelling be mistaken for being Irish and she experience the discrimination that was common toward the Irish at that time. Also in 1920, she built a home with the help of her friend, Vizcaya and Coral Gables architect Phineas Paist. The home was at 2301 Avenue G (later known as 1039 Southwest Second Avenue). This lot, like those adjoining it, was once owned by James Deering, who apparently either sold or gave the property to Altemus. In November of 1920, Paist pulled a permit to construct a frame residence and garage on that property for $800. Presumably, this is the "little green and white cottage" Altemus refers to in "Big Bosses."[25]

It is unclear why Altemus decided to return to Chicago in 1922 after her experience at Vizcaya. The only explanation she provides in the manuscript is that "[l]iving amidst such wealth had ceased to be of interest." Perhaps she desired more independence and a more dynamic urban environment. It appears that she departed on good terms with Deering since he provided her with a letter of recommendation. Yet she had difficulty securing steady lucrative employment in Chicago, and her jobs didn't provide her with the same level of flexibility that she had with Deering. Althea had to make decisions about where to live and what jobs she could take based on the need to care for and educate her son. As a single mother, she clearly had fewer options, both in housing and in work, than other working women in the city.

Altemus provides a window into the experiences of a single working woman and mother, including the bonds formed among working women in the 1920s. Indeed, as more single women entered cities in search of jobs, they helped create female subcultures at the rooming houses, lunch counters, and theaters they frequented. In "Big Bosses" Althea introduced the characters of Nan and Babs as her closest female companions, along with other secretaries like Miss Hewitt at "Town and Malwood" and Miss Stevens, who worked for "Mr. Mack." They helped locate jobs, gave advice for advancement, assisted with child care, and provided much-needed companionship at lunches, teas, and theatrical performances. Altemus discusses the close, almost familial relationships she formed with these women and their children as they shared housing and child-care responsibilities alongside their efforts to secure steady work, pay, and housing. While we know little about her employment in these offices other than what is recounted in "Big Bosses," we do get a sense of the strategies Altemus used to get by.

Throughout the manuscript, Altemus discusses the concerns of male employers with proper displays of femininity and professionalism in the workplace, as well as her own apprehensions over unwanted advances from them. Indeed, some observers of changing office culture worried that the expanding presence of women would threaten the stability of the corporate workplace and of middle-class domestic values. Popular stories in mass-market magazines and novels in the teens and 1920s romanticized office culture and often featured female clerical workers as objects of desire. Clerical workers' office attire became an issue of great interest to social commentators of the day, as appropriate dress was crucial in maintaining proper office culture. Altemus gives firsthand accounts of women using the washrooms in office buildings to take off their wraps and coats and also to remove their wedding rings and put on wigs to cover their bobbed hairdos. "Why 'Big Bosses' demanded the long unsanitary tresses of our grandmothers in this era of evolution was beyond my comprehension," she wrote. The independence and allure of the flapper were exciting and appealing in popular culture, but within the confines of the office, a much more rigid and conservative display of femininity structured working women's lives.[26]

Altemus frequently experienced the injustice of workplace practices that forced working mothers to lie about their motherhood. In "Big Bosses" she lamented, "Whatever crime it is for a woman, who has been left a widow, to wish to earn her own living and keep her child with her, I do not know—but crime it seems to be."[27] She had to face the "marriage bar" that precluded both married women and mothers from obtaining or maintaining employment in most fields, including clerical labor. As "Big Bosses" makes clear, she lived in perpetual fear of her employers discovering that she had a child and terminating her employment, leaving her in a precarious economic position. She appealed to the sentimental side of her potential readers to make a case for fairer and more equitable treatment of working mothers.[28]

Outside of the office, Althea and other women doubtless felt more free. Yet despite this, her own daily routine was shaped by the demands of being a mother. She left parties, dinners, and poker games to get back to the care of her son. She met famous actresses and business leaders, politicians and bootleggers, but always seemed to take the role of observer rather than participant in the action. She referred regularly to her "Scottish" frugalness and strict Presbyterian upbringing, and suggested that those aspects of her background helped her to keep a balanced approach to her work and her life. Yet much of her life was defined by sacrifice and tragedy as a result of the difficult decisions she was forced to make as a single working mother. She and the friends and coworkers she described withstood sexual advances by employers; absent, alcoholic or abusive husbands; limited social networks to sustain them in times of tragedy; the need to leave children to be cared for by others in order to seek employment; and economic insecurity that often threatened their safety and stability. While Altemus's tone generally is light and entertaining, the situations she recounts point to the real difficulties and dangers encountered by working women in urban America.[29]

Just as we do not know for certain why Altemus left Miami in 1922, we also do not know why she returned in 1925, after a brief period in New York. In "Big Bosses," she explained that "everyone in New York was talking of people becoming rich overnight in Miami." A 1924 article in the *Saturday Evening Post* described the real estate speculation shaping Miami's development. "Everyone in South Florida," the article explained, "has just bought a piece of real estate or has just sold a piece of real estate or is on the verge or buying or selling a piece of real estate."[30] Perhaps the lure of lucrative opportunities in Miami prompted the move, along with the difficulties of finding lasting work in New York.

Whatever the reason, Altemus appears to have made a successful life for herself and her son, Robert, back in South Florida. After she returned, she worked as a stenographer for the Barnaby Agency, a real estate firm based in New York that opened branches in South Florida to capitalize on the real estate boom. While the company bought land and had a number of projects slated for development, including in Coral Gables and Miami Beach, few projects were built.[31] By 1928, Altemus had moved to Coral Gables, the planned suburb west of Miami, while she was treasurer of the South Florida Golf and Country Club. By 1930, she was living in the city of Miami once again, renting in at least two different locations; Robert was living with her and studying at Ponce de Leon High School (later Middle School). In 1938, Althea began listing her name in city directories as Mrs. Marie A. Altemus, switching her first and middle names and no longer using her maiden name. It is unclear why she made this change, though perhaps she began using her married name again as she was winding down her professional career. In the 1940 census she indicated that she had worked only thirteen weeks in 1939 and had income from other sources, presumably her son.[32]

Like his mother, Robert worked his way up the business ladder, starting his professional career as a clerk at the Princely Shops and then as a bookkeeper for City Ice and Fuel in 1935. While working, he also took night classes to become a tax specialist. In 1938 his job title was "accountant," and by 1940 he worked in that capacity for the Dade County Commission. Robert's income in 1940 was listed in the census as $5,400 (the equivalent of over $80,000 in 2016 after adjusting for inflation), so he may have begun supporting Althea by 1939 or 1940. Later in 1940, he started working for the accounting firm of Abess, Costar & Roberts. Robert Altemus achieved a great deal of success at the firm. After working there for a year, he purchased his own home in the Shenandoah neighborhood of Miami, close to Coral Gables, and likely helped his mother remain in her home on Southwest Seventh Street, which she had purchased in 1938. Robert achieved partner status in his firm, which eventually took the name of Abess, Morgan, Altemus & Barrs, and later Morgan, Altemus & Barrs. The company became one of the largest accounting firms in Florida, and had clients including the University of Miami and Rocky Marciano, the professional boxer.[33]

Robert's affiliation with firm cofounder Leonard Abess enabled him to achieve success not only in accounting but also in banking. In 1948, Abess and business partner Baron de Hirsch Meyer purchased the Industrial Savings Bank on Flagler Street in Miami. Then, in 1955, they established City National Bank of Coral Gables. By 1959 Altemus was president of that bank, and

Black-and-white photograph of Althea and Robert
Altemus on the porch of her home at 511 Southwest Seventh Street in Miami.

he soon moved with his wife, Rose Marie (Mendelssohn), a typist, to 6600 Southwest 128th Street, in a southern suburb that eventually would become the upscale community of Pinecrest. In addition to raising his sons Robert Wayne and Donald in Pinecrest, Robert also built a home in Burnsville, North Carolina, about forty miles northeast of Asheville. Althea indicated at the end of "Big Bosses" that she had had a cabin in Asheville, so perhaps early trips with his mother inspired Robert to build the home, which remained in his family for quite some time.[34]

We know little about the last decades of Althea's life. Her grandson, Donald Altemus, remembers visiting her at her home on Southwest Seventh Street, sleeping in the screened-in porch and putting trays of ice between him and his older brother, Robert, so they could stay cool. He recalls that in the 1950s she no longer drove, so they frequently did family outings by bus, to the Miracle Theater in Coral Gables, the Olympia Theater in downtown Miami, the Crandon Park Zoo on Key Biscayne, and the Venetian Pool in Coral Gables. The widow of Don's brother, Robert, Tanya Lewicki, remembers her husband speaking fondly about visiting his grandmother and watching trains go by from her porch. He even built an elevated model train track in his home based on this love of trains likely instilled by visits to Althea's house.[35]

When describing his reaction to finding his grandmother's manuscript, Don explained that both he and his brother expressed surprise at the stories she told and the manner in which she told them. They knew her as a very formal, reserved woman. Yet during her later life she apparently was not forthcoming about all of her extraordinary experiences. Their father was similar, according to Don, having a difficult time communicating and being very strict and driven. Don knew little of his father's upbringing, and only vaguely recalled him talking about the connection to Vizcaya. That changed in 1985, when Don chose to get married at Vizcaya, purely because of the estate's beauty rather than any family connection. Yet the wedding prompted his father to open up a bit about his memories of Althea's time there. Robert Sr. even placed a phone call to Vizcaya and spoke with a staff member about his recollections. He talked of riding his bicycle to Vizcaya to wait for Althea to finish work, and of fishing off the barge and catching a boat full of fish and lobster. He recalled Deering's monkeys, Annie and Bertie, and riding the turntable in the automobile garage. He said that he remembered John Singer Sargent painting Deering, and recalled housekeeper Cecelia Adair being a kind woman and architect Phineas Paist being a great storyteller. He also noted that his mother was responsible for the payroll and correspondence, and that Deering always wanted her to have a pencil in her hand.[36]

Don's description of his grandmother's last years suggests that, while she enjoyed her outings with family, she was for the most part a loner. He said that she did not play cards or have other get-togethers with women, and often seemed lonely. Althea died on June 20, 1965, at age seventy-nine, of a ruptured dissecting aortic aneurysm. Her death certificate states that she was found at 132 East Flagler Street, a five-story retail and office building in downtown Miami built in 1925, suggesting that the rupture may have occurred while she was walking or shopping in the city.[37]

It is difficult to reconcile her last quiet, lonely years with the portrait of Althea that emerges in "Big Bosses." Her drive, determination, and sheer perseverance suggest a vivacious, energetic woman taking advantage of all opportunities presented to her. Her experiences of overcoming a difficult marriage, succeeding as a businesswoman, and encountering everyone from industry tycoons to preachers to rumrunners suggests that she led an extraordinary life unlike that of a typical secretary. Moreover, she not only led a remarkable life but chose to recount it in a memoir. Clearly she was a gifted storyteller, and she used her secretarial skills in order to advance her literary aspirations. The stories Altemus shares and the manner in which she tells them incorporate elements from the mass-market magazines surging in popularity at this time, including the *Ladies' Home Journal* and the *Saturday Evening Post*. Regular features of both magazines included practical advice for women, stories about women's changing roles in society, and short romances and adventure stories designed to appeal to an increasingly literate urban population. While there is no way to know if Altemus subscribed to either magazine, the tone of the manuscript and the pace of the storytelling suggest that she was quite conscious of literary tastes in the 1920s and 1930s.[38]

Nor do we know why she ultimately chose not to publish the manuscript. Her grandson Don speculated that it might have been that she did not want the titillating nature of the text to impede her son's rise in the business world. The discovery of her rich memoir offers unique and poignant insight into the daily life of a working woman in 1920s America. The stories it presents throw into sharp focus the enormous benefits of firsthand accounts showcasing the daily, lived experience of those whose voices often are lost to history. Altemus's preface highlights her desire to share her own experiences, a "resume of her adventures, friendships, laughter and heartaches." There is no question that "Big Bosses" is enhanced by the stories it recounts about celebrities and business leaders of the day. But, ultimately, Althea's story is most compelling because it captures so many of the triumphs and tragedies that shape everyday experience and resonate with readers of all backgrounds.

ACKNOWLEDGMENTS

Joel M. Hoffman on behalf of Vizcaya Museum and Gardens
In addition to Robin Bachin's acknowledgments below, Vizcaya
Museum and Gardens feels tremendous gratitude toward Althea
Altemus's grandsons, Donald and Robert Altemus, for their extraordinary generosity in donating the "Big Bosses" manuscript
to our institutional archives. By sharing this document and supporting this project, they have significantly amplified our understanding of James Deering and Vizcaya, and made it possible
for future generations to enjoy their grandmother's intrigu-
ing life story. We also thank Joy Wallace for her characteristic
friendliness and openness that led to our serendipitous meeting with Don Altemus at the Vizcaya Café and Shop in 2012.
And we appreciate the guidance on copyright law that attorney
Rachel Camber provided at the inception of this project. Vizcaya
is enormously grateful to Robin Bachin for the seriousness with
which she studied Althea Altemus and "Big Bosses" and her enlightening and engaging work product. And we join Robin in
thanking University of Chicago Press senior editor Tim Mennel,
editorial associate Rachel Kelly, senior manuscript editor Mark
Reschke, and senior designer Isaac Tobin for their embrace of
and invaluable assistance in completing this book.

Robin F. Bachin

Uncovering and documenting the various characters, adventures, and twists and turns in the life story of Althea McDowell Altemus took a great deal of sleuthing and detective work. Numerous scholars, researchers, archivists, and family members of Altemus provided extraordinary guidance along the way. First and foremost, I am grateful to Joel Hoffman, executive director of Vizcaya Museum and Gardens, for bringing this fascinating and compelling manuscript to my attention and having faith in me to contextualize its significance in Jazz Age American history and the history of women's labor. The staff at Vizcaya were incredibly generous in offering their assistance and making the archival collection, as well as the house itself, completely accessible to me during the research for this book. Former archivist Alex Privee provided preliminary research into Althea Altemus's genealogical background that was incredibly helpful in the early stages of the project. Emily Gibson, Vizcaya's archivist, worked tirelessly to locate documents, images, and stories related to Altemus's time at Vizcaya, and also facilitated the oral history I conducted with Altemus's grandson Don Altemus. Collections assistant Nydia Perez offered a rare, behind-the-scenes tour of Vizcaya that provided great insight into Althea's stories about Vizcaya. Finally, Remko Jansonius, Vizcaya's deputy director for collections and curatorial affairs, answered questions and consulted on a variety of issues throughout the research phase of the project and provided much-needed assistance with images and manuscript preparation in the final stages of production.

I also am incredibly grateful to Don Altemus and his late brother, Robert, for allowing Vizcaya and me to collaborate on sharing their grandmother's memoir with the world. In addition, Don recounted his memories of his grandmother in an oral history interview that helped stitch together some of the pieces of her later life, for which there was little documentation. Tanya Lewicki, the widow of Don's brother, Robert Jr., shared family photographs and stories related to her late husband's memories of his grandmother. Their generosity in providing stories and pictures helped give added depth and breadth to the published memoir.

Sarah Harper Nobles provided outstanding preliminary research for the Chicago portion of the book, identifying sources, tracking down documents, and consulting with archivists and librarians to ensure a thorough recounting of Altemus's time in the Illinois cities of Elgin and Chicago. She also prepared an incredibly helpful timeline of Altemus's life so we could keep track of key dates that often differed from those Altemus presented in the manuscript. Madeline Loshaw provided additional assistance toward the end of the project, filling in gaps and locating sources that helped identify some of the disguised "big bosses."

Numerous librarians and archivists in Chicago helped me navigate the manuscript collections that shed light on Altemus's time there and her relationship to the Deering family and other "bosses." Janet Olson, assistant university archivist at the Deering Library at Northwestern University, provided assistance with the William Deering Family Papers. Amelia Zimet, archives assistant at the Ryerson and Burnham Archives at the Art Institute of Chicago, helped me locate drawings of the Edison Building, where Altemus met with Samuel Insull. At the Newberry Library, Matt Rutherford, curator of genealogy and local history, helped with genealogical research on Althea Altemus and her family, and Gabriella Gione, library assistant at the Roger and Julie Baskes Department of Special Collections, offered assistance with the Chauncey McCormick Papers. Elizabeth Marston, museum director of the Elgin History Museum, conducted research in Elgin High School yearbooks to help determine Altemus's educational background. Melissa Bernasek, director of information services at the Gail Borden Public Library District in Elgin, provided assistance with Elgin City Directory searches, genealogical searches for Althea Altemus and her family, property searches, and news articles in the Elgin National Watch Factory magazine, *The Watch Word*.

Several other archivists outside of Chicago offered essential assistance as well. Lindsey Hillgartner, the reference archivist at the McCormick–International Harvester Collection Library—Archives Division at the Wisconsin Historical Society, helped locate materials related to the merger of the McCormick Harvesting Machine Company and the Deering Harvester Company. Julie A. Ludwig, archivist at The Frick Collection and Frick Art Reference Library Archives, uncovered correspondence related to Altemus's familial connection with the Frick family as well as the relationship between Frick and James Deering. Finally, Rebecca Federman, electronic resources coordinator at the New York Public Library, helped identify jewelers in New York in the 1920s to try to determine the identity of "Tosh."

I also am grateful to the historians with whom I consulted about various components of Altemus's life and the experiences she described. Harold L. Platt, professor emeritus at Loyola University and an expert on the electrification of Chicago, helped confirm the actual identity of "Mr. Mack" to be Samuel Insull. Paul Israel, director and general editor of the Thomas Edison Papers at Rutgers University, and Michele Wehrwein Albion, former curator at the Edison and Ford Winter Estates in Fort Myers, Florida, addressed questions related to Thomas Edison's time in Florida and potential connections to James Deering and

Vizcaya. And Miami historian Arva Moore Parks read portions of the manuscript related to Miami history in the 1920s and offered much-appreciated feedback.

The editors at the University of Chicago Press have been a delight to work with. Senior editor Tim Mennel offered incredibly thorough and thoughtful comments and suggestions that tightened up the manuscript and made it more accessible to readers. He played an active role in every phase of producing this book, and the book is all the better for it. Editorial associate Rachel Kelly, senior manuscript editor Mark Reschke, and senior designer Isaac Tobin have kept the project on track and guided us through its final phases.

Finally, I am grateful to Jorge Kuperman and my children, Marissa and Daniel Coppola, for their patience, support, and encouragement throughout the process of completing this book.

HISTORICAL ANNOTATIONS
AND ENDNOTES

Preface

6

ALL DRAWINGS IN THIS BOOK: Paul Chalfin brought Phineas E. Paist (1873–1937) to Miami in 1916 to serve as on-site project architect in collaboration with F. Burrall Hoffman. At Vizcaya, Paist was responsible for the Casino and many of the staff buildings on the site of the Farm Village, across Miami Avenue from the main house. He also designed the house for James Deering's brother, Charles, who bought property a few miles south of Vizcaya at Cutler. Born in Philadelphia and educated at the Pennsylvania Academy of Fine Arts, Paist received a Cresson Traveling Scholarship for postgraduate studies in Europe, allowing him to travel and study in various cities including Rome, Florence, Orvieto, Venice, and Paris. Upon his return to Philadelphia in 1906, Paist worked in the architectural firm of G. W. and W. D. Hewitt, where he later became partner and helped design Philadelphia's Bellevue Stratford Hotel. After completing his work at Vizcaya, Paist remained in Miami and became a member of the architectural team of the newly planned city of Coral Gables, developed by George Merrick. In Coral Gables, he was the lead colorist, responsible for the pastel hues that would come to define the city's aesthetic, and by 1925 he was named supervising architect for the city. In addition to his work at Vizcaya and in Coral Gables, Paist also designed the Deitrich Commercial Building (1927), the Miami Post Office and Courthouse (1931), and Liberty Square, the first public housing project in Miami (1936). Nicholas N. Patricios, "Phineas Paist and the Architecture of Coral Gables, Florida," *Tequesta* 64 (2004): 5–27; Arva Moore Parks, *George Merrick, Son of the South Wind: Visionary Creator of Coral Gables* (Gainesville, FL: University Press of Florida, 2015), 169–71, 174; Raymond A. Mohl, "Race and Space in the Modern City: Interstate 95 and the Black Community in Miami," in *Urban Policy in Twentieth Century America,* ed. Arnold R. Hirsch and Raymond A. Mohl (New Brunswick, NJ: Rutgers University Press, 1993), 101–56; Witold Rybczynski and Laurie Olin, *Vizcaya: An American Villa and Its Makers* (Philadelphia: University of Pennsylvania Press, 2007), 136–37; John A. Stuart, "Liberty Square: Florida's First Public Housing Project," in *The New Deal in South Florida: Design, Policy, and Community Building, 1933–1940,* ed. John A. Stuart and John F. Stack Jr. (Gainesville: University of Florida Press, 2008), 186–222; "Paist and Steward: Architects," *Architecture and Design* (Miami, FL, 1941), issue housed at Vizcaya Museum and Gardens Archives.

7

ARCHITECTS OF VISCAYA: The trio of Vizcaya "architects" cited by Altemus on her handwritten list includes the chief designer, Paul Chalfin (1874–1959), who meticulously oversaw every aspect of Vizcaya's creation, from site planning to the type of reading lamps in each guest room. Chalfin was a painter educated at Harvard and the École des Beaux-Arts. He worked as a curator at the Boston Museum of Fine Arts and then won a Prix de Rome fellowship to study at the American Academy in Rome. Upon returning to New York, he began working for noted interior designer Elsie de Wolfe. Chalfin first met James Deering when de Wolfe sent Chalfin to Chicago to install a fountain at Deering's home. In 1910, Chalfin and Deering selected the site for Vizcaya, traveled through Italy looking at models for the home, and went on furniture-buying trips throughout Europe. Yet Chalfin was not an architect, and Deering needed a qualified architect with the technical expertise to supervise construction. Deering hired F. Burrall Hoffman Jr. (1882–1980), a New York architect from a prominent family who, like Chalfin, had attended Harvard and the École des Beaux-Arts. He completed an apprenticeship with Carrère and Hastings, the firm that had designed Henry Flagler's Ponce de León Hotel in St. Augustine, where James Deering's parents had a winter home, as well as Flagler's Palm Beach residence, Whitehall. When Deering hired Hoffman, he had been in his own practice just four years. See Rybczynski and Olin, *Vizcaya,* 15–17, 29–33; Kathryn Chapman Harwood, *The Lives of Vizcaya: Annals of a Great House* (Miami, FL: Banyan Books, 1985), 7–11; Paul Chalfin Interview with Robert Tyler Davis, May 1956, Robert Tyler Davis Papers, Smithsonian Institution Archives, RU 7439, Box 4, Folder 20 (hereafter cited as RTD).

7

SECRETARIES - VISCAYA: Altemus lists her role as secretary, bookkeeper, and accountant at Vizcaya from 1916 to 1923. She also lists the locations as Chicago and Miami, suggesting that she started working for Deering in Chicago and then moved to Miami after the completion of Vizcaya's main house, likely at the end of 1917 or in early 1918. James Deering to Paul Chalfin, November 12, 1917, Vizcaya Estate Records, Series 1: Correspondence, Vizcaya Museum and Gardens Archives, hereafter cited as VER; *Polk's Miami City Directory* (Jacksonville, FL: R. L. Polk & Co., 1918).

Wealth

9

THE EX-PRESIDENT OF TEASER AND REAPER: James Deering's father, William, started Deering Harvester Company after moving his family and business interests from Maine to Evanston, Illinois, in 1874. Deering's chief rival in the harvester business was Cyrus H. McCormick, who founded the McCormick Reaper Company in Chicago in 1847. McCormick's son Cyrus Jr. succeeded him as president and then oversaw the merger with Deering, which was controlled by James, his half brother, Charles, and their brother-in-law, Richard Howe. In 1902, J. P. Morgan and Company negotiated the merger and the creation of International Harvester, which became the fourth largest corporation in America behind U.S. Steel, Standard Oil, and the American Tobacco Company. Walter Dill Scott and Robert B. Harshe, *Charles Deering, 1851-1927: An Appreciation Together with His Memoirs of William Deering and James Deering* (Boston: Privately Printed, 1929), Special Collections, Otto G. Richter Library, University of Miami; "International Harvester Chronology," McCormick–International Harvester Collection, Wisconsin Historical Society; "Our Friends, the Deerings," *Evanston Review,* September 6, 1951; "Descendants of William Deering," William Deering Family Papers, Northwestern University Library Archival and Manuscript Collections, Box 1, Folder 2; Rybczynski and Olin, *Vizcaya,* 10-11.

10

FIRST I MUST TELL YOU: James Deering (1859-1925) was born in South Paris, Maine, the second son of William Deering. James's older half brother, Charles, was the son of William and Abby Reed Barbour. After Abby's death in 1856, William married Clara Hamilton, the mother of James and Abby Marion Deering (Howe). James attended Northwestern University and M.I.T. but left to join his father and Charles at the Deering Manufacturing Company in 1880. He served as vice president of International Harvester until 1919, when he formally retired, though he had taken a much less active role in the company years before and devoted himself to art and travel, especially in Paris, where he had a home at Neuilly-sur-Seine. His involvement in promoting close relations between America and France earned him the title of Officer of the Legion of Honor. He served as secretary-treasurer of the Franco-American Committee on Patronage, whose mission was to promote friendly relations between the United States and France. Others who served on the committee included Cyrus McCormick Jr., Robert Todd Lincoln (son of Abraham Lincoln), William Rainey Harper (president of the University of Chicago), and Henry Clay Frick of Carnegie Steel. Deering was a patron of the arts, who served as a director of the Art Institute of Chicago and maintained friendships with many prominent artists, as did his brother, Charles, including John Singer Sargent, Anders Zorn, and Gari Melchers. Scott and Harshe, *Charles Deering, 1851–1927*, 73–76; James Deering to Henry Clay Frick, November 19, 1903, Henry Clay Frick Papers, Series: Correspondence, The Frick Collection/Frick Art Reference Library Archives.

10

HE ADORED ANYTHING AND EVERYTHING FRENCH: In fact, Deering took inspiration from both Italy and France. Vizcaya is modeled after various eighteenth-century Italian villas, including the Villa Rezzonico in Bassano del Grappa, Italy (1670). The interiors featured a seventeenth-century fireplace from Château de Regnéville in France; a 1750s Italian plaster ceiling; wrought iron gates from the Palazzo Pisani in Venice; a sixteenth-century Carrara marble statue of Bacchus, the god of wine; a Louis XV mantel, woodwork, and paneling from Palermo; Ferrarese tapestries from the fifteenth century that hung at poets Robert and Elizabeth Barrett Browning's home in Florence, Italy; and many other exquisite European furnishings. "'Vizcaya,' the Villa and Grounds: A House at Miami, Florida," *Architectural Review* 5, no. 7 (July 1917): 120–67; Rybczynski and Olin, *Vizcaya*, 65–91; *Miami Herald*, March 23, 1915.

12

"WITH ALL MY LOVE, NAN": The lives of Anne and Bertram Winston and James Deering were closely intertwined. Marion Davies, the actress, noted that "Jim [Deering] was very fond of Mrs. Winston." Deering sold land to the Winstons so they could build a home just north of Vizcaya at 2731 Brickell Avenue, which Deering and Chalfin decided were the most agreeable lots. Once the home was built, Vizcaya staff noted that Deering frequently sent flowers and fruit to Mrs. Winston there; they also refer to the meddling of Mrs. Winston in Vizcaya's "domestic arrangements." After

James sold his Paris home, he gave many of its furnishings to the Winstons for their Miami home, and later left Anne additional furnishings in his will. There was a false rumor that James fathered a child with Anne, which started after the Winstons came back from Europe with a child they claimed was their daughter. In fact, Muriel Mason was the daughter of Anne's sister, Mary Odell, and John A. C. Mason, who was arrested in London for passing false checks. Anne and Bertram eventually adopted Muriel. Year: *1910;* Census Place: *Chicago Ward 21, Cook, Illinois;* Roll: *T624_264;* Page: *6B;* Enumeration District: *0940;* FHL microfilm: *1374277;* Year: *1930;* Census Place: *Chicago, Cook, Illinois;* Roll: *483;* Page: *61A;* Enumeration District: *1560;* Image: *861.0;* FHL microfilm: *2340218;* Winston & Co., Bertram M. Winston, William R. O'Dell, real estate and loans, 1414 First National Bank Building, Chicago City Directory, 1915; all from Ancestry.com, *U.S. City Directories, 1822-1995* [database online], Provo, UT: Ancestry.com Operations, Inc., 2011. A. N. Marquis, ed., *The Book of Chicagoans: A Biographical Dictionary of Leading Living Men of the City of Chicago,* vol. 2 (Chicago: A. N. Marquis & Co., 1911), 732; "Chronicles of Eustace," Vizcaya Volunteer Guides Records, Vertical Files, Folder: "Vizcaya People: Edgecombe, Eustace E.," Vizcaya Museum and Gardens Archives; Paul Chalfin Interview with Robert Tyler Davis, May 1956, RTD, Box 4, Folder 20; Chalfin to Deering, October 21, 1919, VER; Deering to Chalfin, October 25, 1919, VER; Chalfin to Louis Koons, January 12, 1920, VER; Deering to Chalfin, October 9, 1920, VER; *The Inter Ocean,* February 3, 1895; April 21, 1895; April 27, 1904; July 3, 1913; *New York Times,* July 10, 1903; Marion Davies, *The Times We Had: Life with William Randolph Hearst,* ed. Pamela Faux and Kenneth S. Marx (Indianapolis: Bobbs-Merrill, 1975), 10-12, 14-15; and "James Deering Last Will and Testament," transcript from *Miami Herald* article circa 1925, Vizcaya Museum and Gardens Archives.

13

NEXT CAME THE DAILY REQUESTS: James Deering donated millions of dollars to charities, in Chicago and Miami, as did his father, siblings, and nieces. He donated $1 million to the Wesley Hospital of Northwestern University in Evanston, Illinois, to assist charity patients, and gave additional gifts to Northwestern for other facilities. Other recipients of his charitable giving included the Visiting Nurse Association of Chicago; the Art Institute of Chicago (including donations of art); and the Miami City Hospital (which became Jackson Memorial Hospital). In his will, Deering also left funds for all of his servants, the amount dependent upon how long they had worked for him. "James Deering Last Will and Testament," transcript from *Miami Herald* article circa 1925, Vizcaya Museum and Gardens Archives; "Our Friends, the Deerings," *Evanston Review,* September 6, 1951; *James Deering* (Chicago: International Harvester Company, 1925), Special Collections, Deering Library, Northwestern University; and Janet Olson, "Roaring through the Twenties: Northwestern Outgrows Its First Library," *Deering Library: An Illustrated History* (Evanston, IL: Northwestern University Press, 2008), 20-21.

15

BEAU MAKE ANOTHER DASH: Deering's health was poor, and he suffered from various stomach ailments most of his adult life. In correspondence, he makes regular reference to his digestive issues. Joseph Santini, the captain of Deering's yachts, talked regularly with him about stomach troubles. Deering would bring his French chef, Theo Cazé, on board the yacht and eat "delicacies," but then spend the next week to ten days "getting right." Paul Chalfin Interview with Robert Tyler Davis, May 1956, RTD, Box 4, Folder 20; Deering to Charles Paul, November 30, 1900, Deering Private Letter Book [5 of 7], McCormick–International Harvester Collection, Wisconsin Historical Society; and Joseph Santini interview by Grace W. Bohne, May 28, 1956, Vizcaya Volunteer Guides Records, Vertical Files, Folder: "Deering Staff," Vizcaya Museum and Gardens Archives.

15

SHE DIDN'T MAKE GOOD: Altemus is referring to Mary Ashley Cleveland, who arrived at Vizcaya in July of 1917. When hiring Cleveland, Deering requested references from all of her previous employers and even wanted to hire a private detective agency to investigate her, though Chalfin advised against the latter. She asked for a salary of $3,000, but Deering agreed to pay her $2,400 plus a lump-sum payment of $600. She initially refused to live at Vizcaya, saying it would appear improper, but Deering insisted. She wished to have complete managerial control over the household. Apparently Deering shared Altemus's assessment of Cleveland, for in the fall of 1918 he hired Ethel Syer to replace her. Museum Records, Subject Files series, Vizcaya Staff Analysis Project, 2006, "Mary Ashley Cleveland" and "Ethel Syer," Vizcaya Museum and Gardens Archives; "Personnel: McCormick, Chauncey," VER.

16

AND IF YOU DON'T THINK THE PARTIES: Harwood, *The Lives of Vizcaya,* 207-10; *Miami Herald,* January 12, 1917; "Paul Chalfin's 'The Blue Dog' is a Unique American House-Boat," *Vanity Fair* 8, no. 5 (July 1917):

56; Rybczynski and Olin, *Vizcaya,* 224–25. Chalfin's boyfriend and business partner, Louis A. Koons, lived with him on the *Blue Dog* and traveled with him on his European art and furniture-buying tours.

16

NOW BEAU THOUGHT EDEN: Chalfin hired Robert Winthrop Chanler to decorate the ceiling of Vizcaya's swimming pool grotto. Chanler wanted the ceiling to be painted to give it a nautical effect, and he designed casts of sea creatures to be placed around the border. Shells for panels on the walls were collected in the Bahamas, and Samuel E. Sands, Vizcaya's "waterboy," sorted through them to select and clean them. In addition, Chanler, who was known for his elaborate screens, produced one for Vizcaya.

Chanler's work caused tension between Deering and Chalfin because Deering said that he wanted to contract with Chanler to do either a screen or the grotto ceiling but not both. Chalfin wrote Deering, "I wish some time that you would write down understandings, as I do, and not carry them in your head," stating that Deering had agreed to both projects. Deering acknowledged that he sometimes had faults of memory, but not in this case. He stated that he and Chalfin "Will say no more about" the episode. This exchange is one example of the sometimes strained and tense relationship between Chalfin and Deering, with Chalfin taking near complete control over all decisions related to Vizcaya's design and Deering often pushing back, particularly with regard to the costs of Chalfin's plans. "Death Comes to Robert Chanler," *Lincoln Star,* October 24, 1930, http://www.newspapers.com/image/58111734; Chalfin to Deering, March 14, 1916, VER; Deering to Chalfin, March 17, 1916, VER; Staff interview notes, Joe Orr, February 17, 1954, RTD, Box 4, Folder 20; and Harwood, *The Lives of Vizcaya,* 233–36.

18

SHE WAS A LOVELY BLONDE: After seeing Marion Davies in a Ziegfeld Follies production, William Randolph Hearst began courting her (despite being married and thirty-four years her senior) and created a film production company, Cosmopolitan Pictures, to promote her acting career. Their relationship was often thought to be the foundation for actor and director Orson Welles's film *Citizen Kane,* though Welles said Kane was based loosely on Samuel Insull, president of Chicago Edison, and his promotion of the career of his actress wife, Margaret Anna Bird (stage name Gladys Wallis). Other accounts have claimed that *Citizen Kane* was inspired by members of the McCormick family of Chicago. See David Nasaw, *The Chief:*

The Life of William Randolph Hearst (Boston: Houghton Mifflin, 2000); Davies, *The Times We Had*, 51, 245n; and Orson Welles and Peter Bogdanovich, *This Is Orson Welles*, ed. Jonathan Rosenbaum (New York: Da Capo Press, 1998), xxv, 49.

18

WE PUT MARY IN THE CHINESE ROOM: Davies claimed that the Cathay Bedroom in which she stayed was called "the Little Princess Room," and said that Deering reserved it for "the younger degeneration." Davies described the room as strange but very nice, with "black marble, pink satin, and ostrich feathers." This description is not far off from that offered by Chalfin, who said the bed in Cathay was "a dream of a Chinese couch as Venice saw it, all parasols and bells and lattice work, carved and lacquered and draped over coralline red, lined with golden yellow, from ostrich plumes and another faded red." Harwood, *The Lives of Vizcaya*, 128-29; Rybczynski and Olin, *Vizcaya*, 86; Davies, *The Times We Had*, 10; and "Vizcaya," *Architectural Review*, 143.

19

A SHORT TIME LATER: Apparently there was some confusion when Davies's gift arrived soon after Christmas of 1919. It was from Cartier and signed "from Marion." Deering thought that the gift was from his niece, Marion Deering McCormick. When he discovered the error, he then asked Chalfin to send a gift to Davies at her Riverside Drive home in New York with a note apologizing for the delay and explaining that he had given Chalfin "imperfect directions for delivery" rather than disclosing the mistake. Deering to Chalfin, January 7, 1919, VER.

19

AT THIS TIME JOHN SARGENT: During his brief stay at Vizcaya in the spring of 1917, John Singer Sargent (1856-1925) painted not only the portrait of Deering but also numerous watercolors depicting the completed portions of the house, such as the patio, terrace, loggia, and basin, and also the Bahamian workers who were in the process of completing the harbor and yacht landing. Rybczynski and Olin, *Vizcaya*, 219-27.

22

MY ILLUSIONS OF THE HEAVENLY BEAUTY: In 1920, prior to the release of *Lessons in Love*, Chalfin received a request for Constance Talmadge to be photographed at Vizcaya. Deering gave reluctant approval, stating that he would "[c]onsent with understanding no similar future requests."

Chalfin thanked Deering and explained that he was expecting to gain a contract to do interior design work for her and this approval would help in that effort. "Constance Talmadge," in *An Encyclopedic Dictionary of Women in Early American Films, 1895–1930* (Binghamton, NY: Haworth Press, Inc.), 2005; Chalfin to Deering, December 7, 1920, VER; Deering to Chalfin, December 8, 1920, VER; and Chalfin to Deering, December 8, 1920, VER.

26

WHEN THE ESTATE WAS DESIGNED: Miami had been "dry" since 1913. In 1915, Deering shipped $27,000 worth of alcohol—labeled "household effects"—from New York to Vizcaya aboard the schooner *Granville R. Bacon*, amid 110 tons of marble for garden statuary. Included in the shipment was Deering's favorite, Cedar Brook Sour Mash Whiskey, along with Spring Hill Bourbon Whiskey, Superior Old Tom Gin, and other liquors. Additional shipments continued through 1916 and 1917, though certain wine and liquor produced in Europe, like vermouth and absinthe, became more difficult to obtain as a result of World War I. In 1919, Chalfin warned Deering that "[t]he liquor situation is tightening up every day, and if you desire these goods, it will be a very simple matter to buy them and store them until the opportune moment arrives of shipping them to Vizcaya." Deering to Chalfin, June 24, 1915, September 4, 1915, and September 22, 1915, VER; Deering to Louis A. Koons, September 10, 1917, and December 12, 1919, VER; Chalfin to Deering, December 26, 1919, VER; Vizcaya Liquor Bottle Inventory, Vizcaya Museum and Gardens Archives; "Spirits of the Ages," typed ms. by Doris B. Littlefield, Vizcaya Volunteer Guides Records, Vertical Files, Folder: "Entertaining," Vizcaya Museum and Gardens Archives; Harwood, *The Lives of Vizcaya*, 74–77.

26

THIS ELABORATE CASINO: W. D. Sturrock to Chalfin, June 2, 1915, VER; Deering to Chalfin, June 18, 1916, June 19, 2016, August 15, 1916, and June 24, 1916, VER; "Spirits of the Ages," typed ms. by Doris B. Littlefield; and Rybczynski and Olin, *Vizcaya*, 116–22.

27

OF COURSE IT WAS MORE ELEVATING: Deering purchased the six-thousand-pound Welte-Mignon pipe organ in 1916 so that it would be installed in time for the official opening of the house on Christmas Eve. Eustace Edgecombe, who occupied numerous jobs at Vizcaya over thirty-five years, was trained to play the pipe organ to accompany the movie screenings held in the courtyard. Deering to Chalfin, September 30, 1913, December 8, 1914, January 14, 1916, and March 20, 1916, VER; Harwood, *The Lives of Vizcaya*, 178–81; "Eustace: Notes on Rooms," Vizcaya Volunteer Guides Records, Vertical Files, Folder: "Vizcaya People: Edgecombe, Eustace E.," Vizcaya Museum and Gardens Archives.

29

IT WAS A DREAMY GROUP: The billiard room that led to the pool featured a billiard table, a hidden bar for storing wine and liquor, and a concealed roulette table. According to Deering, "Though I personally get no fun out of it, I think I am likely to have a roulette table in the establishment. If so, a little partition should be put in the billiard room behind which this can either be operated or at least stored out of sight, for in a community like Miami it would be easy to get an undeserved reputation as a gambler." Deering to F. B. Hoffman, September 27, 1913, VER; Harwood, *The Lives of Vizcaya*, 77.

30

GLENN CURTIS AND HIS LATEST PLANE: In the 1920s, Glenn Curtiss and his family moved to Miami, where he continued his aviation work and became a developer. He created a town designed entirely around scenes from the tales of *The Arabian Nights*, Opa-locka, and also developed the new towns of Hialeah and Miami Springs, the latter designed around a Spanish pueblo architectural theme. C. R. Roseberry, *Glenn Curtiss: Pioneer of Flight* (Syracuse, NY: Syracuse University Press, 1991); Catherine Lynn, "Dream and Substance: Araby and the Planning of Opa-locka," *Journal of Decorative and Propaganda Arts* 23 (1998): 163–88.

31

HE DIDN'T SEE WHY I NEEDED A PACKARD: In October of 1918, Altemus sent a letter to Chalfin asking about the jitney service that took workers back and forth from their homes to Vizcaya. She explained that for her and one of the other female employees, Deering employed a chauffeur, whom he paid $20 per week, to drive them to and from work and pick up the mail. Altemus had proposed to William MacLean, Vizcaya's superintendent, that she drive the car, "which I know how to do well," and also run errands and get the mail, thus saving $20 per week. The response was negative. "Notes from Talk by Eustace Edgewood [*sic*; Edgecombe]," Vizcaya Volunteer Guides Records, Vertical Files, Folder: "Vizcaya People: Edgecombe, Eustace E.," Vizcaya Museum and Gardens Archives; Althea Altemus to Chalfin, October 31, 1918, VER.

31

THEY WERE NEIGHBORS: William Jennings Bryan's property, Villa Ser-
ena, just north of Deering's on Biscayne Bay at 3115 Brickell Avenue, was
designed by noted Miami architect August Geiger. Bryan was a regular guest
at Deering's parties, and both men apparently hosted President Warren
Harding at their homes in April of 1921.

The home James Stanley Joyce built for Peggy at 3031 Brickell became
a point of contention in their well-publicized divorce trial in 1921, as did
the over $1 million worth of jewelry and furs he had given her. Robert W.
Cherny, *A Righteous Cause: The Life of William Jennings Bryan* (Norman:
University of Oklahoma Press, 1994); Harwood, *The Lives of Vizcaya*, 139;
"The Official Plat of the City of Miami" (Miami, FL: Office of the City Engineer: April 1915); *Moving Picture Age* 4 (April 21, 1921); Ivan A. Rodriquez
and W. Carl Shiver, "William Jennings Bryan House," National Register of
Historic Places Registration Form, U.S. Department of the Interior, November 2011; *Pittsburgh Press,* March 21, 1921, and June 19, 1921; and Constance Rosenblum, *Gold Digger: The Outrageous Life and Times of Peggy Hopkins Joyce* (New York: Metropolitan Books/Henry Holt, 2000), 85–89, 115.

35

"WHAT'S SO INTERESTING AT YOUR COTTAGE?": Altemus moved quite
a bit while in Miami, first renting a home at 219 Twelfth Street in 1918, then
buying property at 715 Twentieth Street and then 2301 Avenue G in 1920.
For the latter property, Phineas Paist pulled a permit for a dwelling and
garage, suggesting that he either built the house or made alterations to an
existing structure. It appears that Deering either sold part of his land holdings to Altemus or gave them to her for her home at Avenue G, later 1039
Southwest Second Avenue. Year: *1920;* Census Place: *Miami, Dade, Florida;*
Roll: *T625_216;* Page: *2A;* Enumeration District: *31;* Image: *455; Polk &
Co.'s Miami City Directory* (Jacksonville, FL: R. L. Polk & Co., 1920; 1921;
1922); from Ancestry.com, *U.S. City Directories, 1822–1995* [database online],
Provo, UT: Ancestry.com Operations, Inc., 2011. *Miami Herald,* November 9,
1920, October 12, 1921, and July 22, 1922; G. M. Hopkins & Co., *Plat Book
of Greater Miami, Florida and Suburbs* (Philadelphia: G. M. Hopkins & Co.,
1925), 8, Special Collections, Otto G. Richter Library, University of Miami.

38

WE HAD ENGAGED: "Essay, Private Secretary," Vizcaya Payroll Records,
1912–1924; Chalfin to Deering, September 6, 1919, VER; Deering to Chalfin, September 10, 1919, and October 1, 1919, VER.

Chicago

39

WE HAD GIVEN THE ONCE OVER: "Marshall Field & Company," in *The Electronic Encyclopedia of Chicago* (Chicago: Chicago Historical Society, 2005).

40

ST. JOSEPH'S HOSPITAL ON THE NORTHSIDE: The Daughters of Charity (who had merged with the Sisters of Charity of St. Joseph) founded St. Joseph Hospital in 1868 in Lakeview. Two years later, they built a new hospital at Burling and Dickens Streets. "Hospitals" and "Overview/History: Presence St. Joseph Hospital," in *The Electronic Encyclopedia of Chicago.*

40

I DIDN'T LIKE THAT IDEA: The "marriage bar" shaped women's job opportunities in the office workforce. It stipulated that women could work until they married, at which point they would lose their jobs. There were a variety of rationales for this rule. Employers and male labor unions alike argued that once women were married, they had a husband who would earn a family wage, making the woman's wage earning unnecessary. Similarly, employers expressed concern that women would become more devoted to their husbands than to their jobs, and even more so to their eventual children. This bar allowed employers to create a separate career path for women, since there would be no expectation that women would advance and move to higher-ranking positions, thereby providing a steady flow of relatively low-wage office workers. As a result, clerical labor became more segmented and differentiated by gender. The marriage and child bar held both for entry-level clerical positions and for the most desirable jobs like private secretary, the positions held and sought by Altemus. Still, by 1930, close to 20 percent of all female office workers were married. See Aimee Buchanan, *The Lady Means Business: How to Reach the Top in the Business World—the Career Woman's Own Machiavelli* (New York: Simon and Schuster, 1942), 111; Jerome P. Bjelopera, *City of Clerks: Office and Sales Workers in Philadelphia, 1870-1920* (Urbana: University of Illinois Press, 2005), 64-65; Margery W. Davies, *Woman's Place Is at the Typewriter: Office Work and Office Workers, 1870-1930* (Philadelphia: Temple University Press, 1982), 79-96; Lisa M. Fine, *The Souls of the Skyscraper: Female Clerical Workers in Chicago, 1870-1930* (Philadelphia: Temple University Press, 1990), 31-34, 51-54, 96-103; Sharon Hartman Strom, *Beyond the Typewriter: Gender, Class, and the Origins of Modern American Office Work, 1900-1930* (Urbana:

University of Illinois Press, 1992), 8, 190–96, 388; and Lynn Y. Weiner, *From Working Girl to Working Mother: The Female Labor Force in the United States* (Chapel Hill: University of North Carolina Press, 1985), 98–110.

41

TOWN & MALWOOD: The name of the firm at which Altemus worked is disguised. A survey of patent attorneys in Chicago in the 1920s yielded some firms with names that slightly resemble Town and Malwood. One of the largest patent attorney firms in Chicago was Poole and Brown, established in the 1880s. Their offices were located in the Marquette Building, at 140 South Dearborn, home to numerous patent attorneys. A. N. Marquis, ed., *The Book of Chicagoans: A Biographical Dictionary of Leading Living Men of the City of Chicago*, vol. 2 (Chicago: A. N. Marquis & Co., 1911), 513, 545; *Blue Book of Chicago Commerce, 1920* (Chicago: Chicago Association of Commerce & Industry, 1920), 565; J. Seymour Currey, *Chicago: Its History and Builders*, vol. 4 (Chicago: S. J. Clarke Publishing Co., 1918), 299–300; "Col. T. E. Brown, Lawyer and '98 Veteran, Is Dead," *Chicago Daily Tribune*, April 2, 1927; and "Annie Poole, Daughter of Library Founder, Is Dead," *Chicago Daily Tribune*, October 31, 1930.

41

THE JOB WAS MINE: By the 1920s, there was a growing expectation that clerical workers should have at least a high school degree, having taken some courses in business or communication. Increasingly, college-educated women also entered the clerical workforce. Yet many female college graduates found that there were few jobs available to them upon graduation. More senior clerical positions like professional secretary became an option for many who found the doors to other professions, including law, medicine, banking, and advertising, closed to them despite their college degrees. Strom, *Beyond the Typewriter*, 336–42; Davies, *Woman's Place Is at the Typewriter*, 71–78.

41

INTO THE PERSONAL COLUMN: This ad highlights the importance for single working mothers of finding adequate housing and good child care, as there were few affordable housing options for women with children. While various women's organizations started rooming houses explicitly for single women, like the Eleanor Residences in Chicago, few provided accommodations for women and their children. See Fine, *Souls of the Skyscraper*, 41–42, 152–53; Joanne J. Meyerowitz, *Women Adrift: Independent Wage Earners in Chicago, 1880–1930* (Chicago: University of Chicago Press, 1988), chapters

4 and 5; and Jeanne Catherine Lawrence, "Chicago's Eleanor Clubs: Housing Working Women in the Early Twentieth Century," *Perspectives in Vernacular Architecture*, vol. 8, *Vernacular Architecture Forum* (2000): 219-47.

42

NITA WAS CONVERSANT: Nita's story highlights the difficulties working women faced in being alone in the city. Many urban reformers feared that single women in the city could fall prey to confidence men who would promise them gifts and other luxuries that they were unable to obtain on their own. In doing so, the women could be lured into various forms of vice, including prostitution. A report by the Chicago Vice Commission in 1911 told the story of a former salesgirl at a Chicago department store whose "eyes had been opened to her earning capacity in the 'sporting' life by a man who laughed at her for wasting her good looks and physical charms behind a counter." Theodore Dreiser's *Sister Carrie* featured a young woman from the country encountering the lures of urban life and falling victim to men who promised riches and finery that her meager salary did not afford her. Altemus's tale of Nita incorporates some of these elements of the lure of luxury, as well as the mysteries of how it was obtained. Vice Commission of Chicago, *The Social Evil in Chicago: A Study of Existing Conditions with Recommendations of the Vice Commission of Chicago* (Chicago: Gunthorp-Warren, 1911), 202, 204; Theodore Dreiser, *Sister Carrie* (New York: Dover, 2004 [1900]); Meyerowitz, *Women Adrift*, 73-77; and Kathy Peiss, *Cheap Amusements: Working Women and Leisure in Turn-of-the-Century New York* (Philadelphia: Temple University Press, 1986); Daphne Spain, *How Women Saved the City* (Minneapolis: University of Minnesota Press, 2002), 43-44.

45

SHE USUALLY LUNCHED: Elbert Hubbard, *A Little Journey to the Hotel Sherman* (East Aurora, NY: The Roycrofters, 1915); "Hotels," in *The Electronic Encyclopedia of Chicago*; Frank A. Randall, *History of the Development of Building Construction in Chicago* (Urbana: University of Illinois Press, 1949), 43; "New College Inn Opens in the Sherman Tuesday," *Chicago Tribune*, September 3, 1967.

48

THOSE WILSON PATENTS: Chicago became central to the manufacture of baseball gloves and balls due to the accessibility of the leather and hides that were by-products of the meatpacking industry, located at the Union Stockyards on the South Side of Chicago. In 1922, Wilson patented the

Ray Schalk catcher's mitt, designed for the legendary Chicago White Sox catcher. This could have been the project on which Altemus was working, since she indicates that she is working for "Town and Malwood" in 1922. "Sporting Goods Manufacturing" and "Wilson & Co.," in *The Electronic Encyclopedia of Chicago;* Gerald R. Gems, *Windy City Wars: Labor, Leisure and Sport in the Making of Chicago* (Lanham, MD: Scarecrow Press, 1997); and Steven A. Riess, *Touching Base: Professional Baseball and American Culture during the Progressive Era* (Urbana: University of Illinois Press, 1999).

49

I MET HIM AT DE JOGHNE'S: Randall, *History of the Development of Building Construction,* 86; *Chicago Tribune,* February 28, 1938; "The Heavenly Recipe That Helped Make Henri de Jonghe Immortal," *Chicago Tribune,* January 27, 1985.

50

AN OFFICER PUSHED US BACK: There are numerous accounts of "vampire cars" mysteriously striking nighttime pedestrians in Chicago in the 1920s. See, for example, "One Woman, Two Men Killed by 'Vampire' Cars," *Chicago Daily Tribune,* December 5, 1921.

52

THE NURSE TOLD ME LATER: Whether this episode occurred or not is impossible to verify. Yet the story reads like a cautionary tale for Altemus and other working women, given that Nita claims to have been a stenographer who lost numerous jobs as a result of being a mother. The story illustrates the difficulties and potential tragedies that could befall single working mothers in the 1920s.

55

MICKELBERRY'S SAUSAGE: The Mickelberry Sausage Factory was located at Forty-Ninth Place and Halsted Street. The company originated in the South and began distributing its sausages to railroad cars and stores throughout the country. After the firm launched a newspaper advertising campaign, orders poured in, and they opened sausage factories in other locations, including Chicago. The factory suffered damage from a fire that broke out from an explosion on a gasoline truck in February of 1968. "Advertises after 25 Years, Gets 1,382 Dealers in 14 Days," *Marketing Communications* 118 (1922): 17–18; "Death Toll Goes Up to 8," *Chicago Tribune,* February 9, 1968.

57

HER PHYSICIAN, DR. LERNER: There is no Dr. Lerner listed in medical directories for Chicago in the 1920s. Ravenswood Hospital was founded in 1905 and, by 1921, had capacity to care for 1,600 patients. See *History of Medicine and Surgery and Physicians and Surgeons of Chicago* (Chicago: Biographical Publishing Corporation, 1922), 312.

59

IF CAPONE COULD HAVE SEEN: Dominic A. Pacyga, *Chicago: A Biography* (Chicago: University of Chicago Press, 2009), 245; "Al Capone," "Crime and Chicago's Image," in *The Electronic Encyclopedia of Chicago*.

Pierre Duval

62

PIERRE DUVAL: There is no record of a Pierre Duval in any city directories or business directories of Chicago in the 1920s. The only architect with a French-sounding name was Louis C. Bouchard, yet his biography does not match Altemus's description of Duval. "Louis Bouchard," *Construction News* 40, no. 1 (July 3, 1915); "Louis Bouchard," *American Contractor* 42 (January 22, 1921); and Susan O'Connor Davis, *Chicago's Historic Hyde Park* (Chicago: University of Chicago Press, 2013), appendix 375.

Sleuths

71

GEORGE ARLISS' MAN WHO PLAYED GOD: "Movie Review: The Man Who Played God," *New York Times*, February 11, 1932.

74

ONE OF CHICAGO'S GENERAL UTILITIES MAGNATES: Samuel Insull, president of Commonwealth Edison, was likely the model for "Hasbeen's" husband. Insull was born in London and became the private secretary of Thomas A. Edison's representative there, George E. Gouraud. In 1881, Insull moved to New York to become Edison's own private secretary. In 1889 he became general vice president of the Edison General Electric Company, later General Electric. Insull moved to Chicago in 1892, where he became president of Chicago Edison. In 1897, Insull incorporated Commonwealth

Electric Light and Power, and in 1907 the two companies merged to become Commonwealth Edison.

Insull first saw his future wife, Gladys, in Chicago in 1893 when she was performing at the McVicker's Theater during the World's Columbian Exposition. They met formally at a dinner party in 1897 and married in 1899. The couple maintained a fashionable residence at 1100 Lake Shore Drive (where Altemus likely met her for the initial appointment) as well as a country home in Libertyville, a suburb of Chicago. John F. Wasik, *The Merchant of Power: Samuel Insull, Thomas Edison, and the Creation of the Modern Metropolis* (New York: Palgrave Macmillan, 2006), 75–76; Forrest McDonald, *Insull: The Rise and Fall of a Billionaire Utility Tycoon* (Chicago: University of Chicago Press, 1962), 74–101; Harold L. Platt, *The Electric City: Energy and the Growth of the Chicago Area, 1880–1930* (Chicago: University of Chicago Press, 1991), 59–92; and Samuel Insull Papers, 1799–1970, Loyola University Chicago Archives.

74

'HE IS NO LONGER INTERESTED': There was tension in Samuel and Gladys's marriage for quite some time, becoming especially acute after Samuel Junior (1900–1983) became ill with scarlet fever in January of 1912. Three nurses cared for him in the Libertyville home, where he was supposed to be quarantined. Samuel Sr. returned to their Gold Coast home, but Gladys stayed in Libertyville. Junior finally recovered in April. During that time, the relationship between Gladys and Samuel Sr. grew more and more strained. According to one biographer, Gladys effectively ended the intimate part of their relationship then, which had been dormant for quite some time before. She complained that Insull was more devoted to his work than to her. She also appeared to suffer from anxiety and depression; Insull later wrote his son: "I am sorry to say your mother has not been at all well—her nerves are in very bad shape and she is very much depressed." Samuel Insull to Samuel Insull Jr., April 11, 1916, Insull Papers, Box 1, Folder 5. Letters from Junior to his mother make regular reference to her "illness" and suffering. Insull Papers, Box 7, Folders 1 and 2; McDonald, *Insull*, 145–48.

75

'NOW I HAVE LIVED WITH MR. MACK': It is interesting that Gladys refers to Insull as "Mack" in light of similarities between Insull's marital story and that of Harold Fowler McCormick, son of Cyrus McCormick. After divorcing his first wife, Edith Rockefeller McCormick, in 1921, McCormick married opera singer Ganna Walska in 1922 and actively promoted her career despite her lack of critical acclaim. Similarly, Samuel Insull helped revive Gladys's acting career by promoting her work as actor-director of the Studebaker Theater in Chicago from 1926 until its demise in 1931. The McCormicks and the Insulls were neighbors on Lake Shore Drive, and the McCormicks had a country house in Lake Forest, near Libertyville. And both men were patrons of opera, with McCormick providing significant funding for the Chicago Civic Opera and Insull building the forty-five-story Civic Opera House at 20 North Wacker Drive in 1929.

76

"MR. MACK HAS A BEAUTIFUL SUITE": Previously, the Edison Company offices were located at 120 West Adams until they outgrew that space. It took several years to move all operations into the new space, with the library not moving until 1915, but Insull's private offices were the first to relocate there. Randall, *History of the Development of Building Construction*, 230; *Architectural Review* 38 (July 1915); *Inland Architect* 49 (June 1907); and "Interview with Miss Helen Norris," July 16, 1958, Forrest McDonald Papers, Loyola University Chicago Archives, Box 3, Folder 12.

79

AUDITORIUM ANNEX: "Auditorium Annex," Historic American Building Survey, HABS No. ILL-1012, National Park Service, 1962; Randall, *History of the Development of Building Construction*, 135.

83

A PERFORMANCE OF ROSE MARIE: Elliott Robert Barkan, ed., *Making It in America: A Sourcebook on Eminent Ethnic Americans* (New York: ABC-CLIO, 2001), 129; "Rudolf Friml," in *The Encyclopedia of Popular Music*, vol. 3, ed. Colin Larkin (London: Muse, 1998), 2036.

89

HOFFMAN HOUSE: Thomas Edison and his family moved to New York City in 1881 and soon lived in an annex to the Clarendon Hotel on Union Square. Edison never lived at the Hoffman House, though the Hoffman House did have an annex like the Clarendon Hotel, and Edison did favor Hoffman House cigars, which continued to be manufactured after the hotel's demise. Several letters and telegrams in Edison's personal papers mention his fondness for the cigars and include requests from his second wife, Mina, to their son Theodore to purchase some for his father. Paul Israel, *Edison: A Life of Invention* (New York: John Wiley & Sons, Inc., 1998),

121–24 and 230–33; Randall Stross, *The Wizard of Menlo Park: How Thomas Alva Edison Invented the Modern World* (New York: Crown, 2007), 39–46; Theodore M. Edison to Hoffman House Cigars, February 6, 1925, Edison Family Papers, Charles Edison Fund Collection, Rutgers University.

90

"YOUR LAST GUESS IS CORRECT": Thomas Edison was one of James Deering's distinguished visitors. In his handwritten notes from his interview with Paul Chalfin, Vizcaya director Robert Tyler Davis notes that "Thos. Edison was one of 'most bores' [?] to visit Vizcaya," though the phrase "most bores" is difficult to read. Paul Chalfin Interview with Robert Tyler Davis, May 1956, Handwritten notes, RTD. Edison may have been part of Warren Harding's traveling party that visited Vizcaya in April of 1921. *Moving Picture Age* 4 (April 1921): 32.

93

THE PRESIDENT LED THE WAY: Ryerson and Burnham Archival Image Collection, Ryerson and Burnham Libraries, Art Institute of Chicago.

97

FLORENCE BECAME VERY SERIOUS: Florence's story may be a stand-in for Althea's own. It is curious that Altemus repeats "Florence's" story about losing her son but says nothing about her own experience with a similar tragedy. Perhaps Florence's explanation that she sought out "forgetfulness in the less serious life of a big city" in part explains Altemus's story as well.

105

INTERESTED IN SPIRITUALISM: The spiritualism movement began in the United States during the period of the Second Great Awakening in the 1840s, in which religious zeal swept over regions of the country, particularly upstate New York. Spiritualism spread throughout the United States and into England and other parts of Europe. Séances were held by those purporting to be mediums, and many prominent people, including Mary Todd Lincoln, wife of the slain president; utopian socialist thinker Robert Owen; and Chicago journalist William T. Stead, became proponents. Bret E. Carroll, *Spiritualism in Antebellum America* (Bloomington: Indiana University Press, 2007), 248; Ann Braude, *Radical Spirits: Spiritualism and Women's Rights in Nineteenth-Century America* (Bloomington: Indiana University Press, 2001), 296.

107

THE BOOK WAS ONE WRITTEN: Arthur Conan Doyle's books on spiritualism included *The New Revolution* (1916), *The Vital Message* (1919), and
Wanderings of a Spiritualist (1921), which may be the book that Altemus
gave "Hasbeen." Andrew Lycett, *The Man Who Created Sherlock Holmes: The
Life and Times of Sir Arthur Conan Doyle* (New York: Free Press, 2008), 400–
430.

Phylander & Company

108

MY NEXT ENGAGEMENT: "Phylander & Co." was the firm of stockbrokers Raymond, Pynchon & Co., whose Chicago offices were at the Rookery
Building at 209 South La Salle Street, designed by Burnham and Root in
1886. The building was home to the Corn Exchange Bank, the Illinois Trust
& Savings Bank, and stockbrokers, bankers, and agents, given its proximity
to the Board of Trade. It is interesting to note that Altemus comments on
this employer's kindness and generosity, and his acceptance of her role as a
mother. Raymond, Pynchon & Co. partner H. D. Sturtevant was featured in
a story in the *Chicago Tribune* in 1913 for petitioning to adopt a relative of
his wife's whom they had taken in as a baby. The petition to formally adopt
him meant that Sturtevant's entire estate would eventually be left to the
child, suggesting that he perhaps more than other bosses would be sympa-
thetic to Altemus's motherhood. *Board of Trade, Stock Exchange and Bankers'
Directory* (Chicago: Financial Pub. Co., 1897); *Polk's Chicago Directory* (Jacksonville, FL: R. L. Polk & Co., 1923); Randall, *History of the Development of
Building Construction*, 112, 152; and *Chicago Tribune*, September 4, 1913.

112

HAD SUDDENLY PASSED AWAY: Althea and her son "Bobbie" are listed
in the obituary. McDowell was buried at the Bluff City Cemetery in Elgin.
"Charles McDowell Obituary," *The Watch Word*, June 1923; "Illinois Deaths
and Stillbirths, 1916–1947," index, *FamilySearch* (https://familysearch.org
/pal:/MM9.1.1/N3FZ-HL2: accessed June 26, 2014), Charles J. Mcdowell,
May 27, 1923; citing Public Board of Health, Archives, Springfield, IL; FHL
microfilm 1557115.

Country

113

SHE PROGRESSED TO THE DRAKE HOTEL: William R. Host and Brooke Alme Portman, *Early Chicago Hotels* (Charleston, SC: Arcadia Publishing, 2006), 79–85; John W. Stamper, *Chicago's North Michigan Avenue: Planning and Development, 1900–1930* (Chicago: University of Chicago Press, 1991), 118–21; and Randall, *History of the Development of Building Construction,* 255.

New York

117

LIKE ALL NICE GIRLS: Opened in 1903, between Park and Madison Avenues, the hotel had 450 rooms and shared baths on every floor. It also included a drug store, a ladies' tailor shop, a manicurist, a ladies' shoe polishing parlor, and a newsstand. One article about the hotel explained that its tenants were "teachers, bookkeepers, stenographers, musicians, artists, writers, nurses, physicians and other professional women." Paul Groth, *Living Downtown: The History of Residential Hotels in the United States* (Berkeley: University of California Press, 1994), chap. 4; Kathy Peiss, *Cheap Amusements,* 34–55; "Martha Washington Hotel," Landmarks Preservation Commission, June 12, 2012, Designation List 456; and "Hotel for Women Only," *New York Times,* February 3, 1903.

117

I THINK ITS JUST SPLENDID: "Jetta Goudal," "Constance Talmadge," in *An Encyclopedic Dictionary of Women in Early American Films;* "Jetta Goudal Suffers Breakdown," *New York Times,* May 24, 1930.

119

I BECAME PRIVATE SECRETARY: This employer is likely Harry S. Black. Born in Ontario, Canada, Black moved to the United States at a young age and started working for George A. Fuller, a prominent architect who moved from New York to Chicago in 1882. Black married Fuller's daughter, Allon Mae, in 1894, and Fuller took him on as a vice president. Upon Fuller's death in 1900, Black became president of the company and quickly expanded its reach and holdings, merging several construction firms to create the U.S. Realty and Construction Company, the predecessor to USRIC. The company, both under Fuller and later under Black, was responsible for

numerous notable buildings, including in Chicago the Tacoma Building
(1888), the Rookery Building (1888), and the Monadnock Building (1889),
and in New York, the Flatiron Building (1902), Pennsylvania Station (1910),
the New York Times Building (1912), and the Plaza Hotel (1907). Black had
a residence in Palm Beach and frequently came to Miami, where he was a
luncheon guest of James Deering's in March of 1915. Black was arrested on
two separate occasions for bootlegging in Miami, including in 1921 when
his private car containing a large quantity of whiskey was seized in Coconut
Grove. "Fuller (George A.) Co.," in *The Electronic Encyclopedia of Chicago;*
Thomas Leslie, *Chicago Skyscrapers, 1871-1934* (Urbana: University of Illinois Press, 2013); Sarah Landau and Carl Condit, *The Rise of the New York
Skyscraper, 1865-1913* (New Haven, CT: Yale University Press, 1996), 301;
Miami Herald, March 3, 1919; and "Jurors Sample Whisky, Then Free Harry
Black," *New York Times,* March 25, 1921.

119

IT SEEMS HIS FIRST WIFE: This part of the story does not exactly match
Black's life. After several separations from Black, his first wife, Allon Mae
Fuller Black, filed suit for divorce in 1905 and married Tyler Morse of Boston in 1906. When Allon died on October 10, 1915, her estate was estimated
to be worth over $5 million, most of it inherited from her father. Half of
the estate was left to Black as trustee of her nephew, George Alton Fuller,
for whom the couple cared while they were married and whom Black later
adopted. In addition, Black was paid $250,000 in fulfillment of an agree-
ment entered into on December 8, 1894. In March of 1922, Black became
engaged to Isabelle Louise May, daughter of a prominent Washington, DC,
family. They married in June of 1922, when Black was fifty-nine and May
was thirty-nine. While the circumstances Altemus reports here mention
only the death of Black's first wife but not the divorce, Black, like Altemus,
may not have been forthcoming about the divorce, especially since Allon
was the one who filed for it. "Divorce, Shares Morse Millions," *New York
Tribune,* October 19, 1915; "Isabelle L. May Is Engaged to Harry S. Black,"
New York Tribune, March 22, 1922.

120

OUR WORK IN THIS OFFICE: Black was a member of numerous prominent social clubs, including the Metropolitan, Manhattan, New York Yacht,
and the Turf and Field Clubs. He served on the board of governors of many,
including the Metropolitan Club, and helped recruit new members. "Manhattan Club Opposition Wins," *New York Times,* May 17, 1922; *New York
Times,* July 20, 1930.

120

THIS "BIG BOSS" COULD NEVER EAT LUNCH: Harry Black was known to suffer from a nervous condition and depression, and in October of 1929 he was found unconscious in the bathtub at his Plaza Hotel penthouse suite by his valet. A "pulmotor crew" saved his life after nine hours spent trying to resuscitate him. He had been ill for several weeks, with acute indigestion and other ailments, and was under the care of a nurse. "H. S. Black, Stricken in Bathtub, Better," *New York Times*, October 20, 1929.

120-121

THEN ONE DAY THIS BIG BOY: This is another instance in which the story does not conform to the facts of Black's life. He and his second wife, Isabelle, did not have any children. According to the *New York Times*, "Mr. Black left no notes, and no explanation of his act was forthcoming." In the day following his death, there were reports that his suicide was caused by losses in the stock market. Black's nephew, George Alton Fuller, denied that financial worries prompted the suicide, and the USRIC issued a statement revealing that the company was financially healthy. The coroner declared that the motive for the suicide was "melancholia." At the time of Black's death, his wife, Isabelle, was traveling in Ireland, and the funeral was delayed to await her return. "H. S. Black Ends Life by Bullet in Home; No Motive Revealed," *New York Times*, July 20, 1930; "Melancholia Given as Black's Motive," *New York Times*, July 21, 1930.

121

ENRY HAY HICK'S DAUGHTER ELLEN: Adelaide Howard Childs, Henry Clay Frick's wife and Helen Clay Frick's mother, had five siblings from her father's first marriage; one of them was Lyman Beecher Childs. Childs married Annie Levy, the sister of Medora Louise Levy Altemus, who was the mother of Althea Altemus's husband, Wayne. Lyman Beecher Childs, then, was the uncle of both Helen Clay Frick and Wayne Altemus. After Annie died in 1912, Childs lived in the Altemus household in Philadelphia for a brief time while Althea and Wayne were living there as well. Martha Frick Symington Sanger, *Helen Clay Frick: Bittersweet Heiress* (Pittsburgh: University of Pittsburgh Press, 2008), xii, 6–8; Eleanor Ward Altemus, "History of the Descendents [*sic*] of Johann Friederich Althomus, Known in America as Frederick Altemus," (1987), 8–9, typescript provided to author by Donald Altemus, housed at Vizcaya Museum and Gardens Archives. James Gopsill, *Gopsill's Philadelphia City Directory for 1890*, Philadelphia: James Gopsill's Sons, 1891; Thirteenth Census of the United States, 1910: Population, Philadelphia, Pennsylvania; Year: *1880;* Census Place: *Philadelphia, Pennsyl-*

vania; Roll: *1186;* Family History Film: *1255186;* Page: *142B;* Enumeration District: *577;* Image: *0284;* 1909 Boyd's Philadelphia city directory; Family History Library; United States & Canada Film 1606070; all from Ancestry .com, *Philadelphia City Directory, 1890* [database online], Provo, UT: Ancestry.com Operations Inc., 1998.

121

I KNEW THE FUTILITY: Lyman Beecher Childs sent several appeals to his brother-in-law Henry Clay Frick between 1909 and 1913 asking for Frick's assistance in projects related to the Altemus Manufacturing Company, which made automotive ignition parts. In one instance, he requested a loan of $10,000 to help the company produce a specialty ignition apparatus. In a letter dated October 5, 1909, Childs tells Frick that he spoke with his sister Addie (Frick's wife Adelaide), who informed him that Frick never received his first correspondence from the previous month. There is no response on record. In 1911 and again in 1913, Childs asks Frick to recommend that U.S. Steel use a paint that the Altemus Company produced. Frick responds by saying that he is unable to do anything about the request. Lyman Beecher Childs to Henry Clay Frick, October 5, 1909 and September 19, 1913; Frick to Childs, December 12, 1911, Henry Clay Frick Papers, Series: Correspondence, The Frick Collection/Frick Art Reference Library Archives.

122

MY LETTER TO MISS HICK: Helen Clay Frick wrote a letter to Charlotte Altemus, Wayne's sister, thanking her for sending a photograph of her mother, Adelaide, as a young girl. There is no record of correspondence between Althea and Helen, however, nor is there any evidence that Adelaide visited Vizcaya. Henry Clay Frick and James Deering were connected, though, as a result of Deering's invitation to Frick to serve on the Franco-American Committee on Patronage, an organization whose purpose was to facilitate friendship and encourage intellectual, industrial, and financial relations between the two countries. Frick agreed to serve. James Deering to Henry Clay Frick, November 19, 1903; Frick to Deering, December 4, 1903, Henry Clay Frick Papers, Series: Correspondence, The Frick Collection/Frick Art Reference Library Archives.

Struber & Company

123

THE BUSY BANKING HOUSE: "Struber" was Simon William Straus, who first worked with his father in the Chicago branch of Straus Bros. & Co., and then created the S. W. Straus Company in 1894. In 1915, Straus moved to New York and was responsible for financing the Ziegfeld Theater, the New York Athletic Club, and the Chrysler Building, which at the time of Straus's death in 1930 was the world's tallest building. In Chicago, the company financed over four thousand buildings, including their own office building on the site of the former Stratford Hotel at Michigan Avenue and Jackson Street. The Straus Building, completed in 1924, was the first building in Chicago with more than thirty floors. Straus was a noted philanthropist who gave money to the Federation for the Support of Jewish Philanthropic Societies, the Jewish Charities of Chicago, and Beth Israel Hospital. He also was a promoter of thrift education, and founded the Society to Teach the American People Thrift. "Simon William Straus," in Marquis, ed., *The Book of Chicagoans;* "$12,000,000 Deal Closed," *New York Times,* December 3, 1922; "Society Founded to Teach the American People Thrift," *New York Times,* November 2, 1913; "Funeral Today for S. W. Straus, Banker, Philanthropist," *Jewish Telegraphic Agency,* September 9, 1930; and S. W. Straus, *History of the Thrift Movement in America* (Philadelphia: J. B. Lippincott, 1920).

124

AFTER DISCARDING WRAPS: Clerical workers' office attire became an issue of great concern to social commentators of the day, as proper dress and appearance were crucial in maintaining respectable office culture. Clerical workers were supposed to look womanly, so that work could not be seen as a threat to femininity, but they could not be too sexy, lest they distract male workers. Bobs were forbidden as they were associated with the look of the flapper and were not considered professional. Jessie R. Wilson, the personnel manager at Curtis Publishing (the Philadelphia company that published some of the most prominent magazines in the 1920s including the *Ladies' Home Journal* and the *Saturday Evening Post*), helped design the dress code, which became standard for offices across the country. Women were barred from wearing a "peek-a-boo" shirtwaist because revealing blouses "invited unwelcome advances from some of their men associates as well as the disapproval of supervisors and other girls with whom they worked." According to Wilson, all office workers should avoid "eccentricity and informality," and she urged young women to peruse fashion sections of magazines, especially the *Ladies' Home Journal*, to get ideas for office dress. Jan Cohen, *Creating America: George Horace Lorimer and the Saturday Evening Post* (Pittsburgh: University of Pittsburgh Press, 1989); Helen Damon-Moore, *Magazines for the Millions: Gender and Commerce in the Ladies' Home Journal and the Saturday Evening Post, 1880–1910* (Albany: State University of New York Press, 1994).

125

BUILDINGS WERE GOING UP: Straus attested to the rapid growth of the building industry and the role of real estate bonds in promoting it when he said, "The rapid development of our business . . . is really significant of the growth of the building industry. . . . As I look into the future it is my belief that we are approaching an era of development in this country which will far surpass anything witnessed before." "$12,000,000 Deal Closed," *New York Times*, December 3, 1922.

129

HE WAS BEING WHEELED AROUND: James Deering's poor health meant that he often took trips to spas for "rest cures." In June of 1920, he stayed at the Hôtels du Parc et Majestic in Vichy, France, for a month, with plans to stay for another month. He reported, "I am feeling pretty well, but the place or the cure does not seem to be good for my nerves." In October of 1917, he went to the Elms Hotel in Excelsior Springs, Missouri, because the spa was supposed to be "good for the digestive tract." During the early phase of the construction of Vizcaya, Deering asked Chalfin if there would be accommodations made for a wheelchair in the house, and he used the chair often to move through the grounds. Deering to Chalfin, June 14, 1920, October 25, 1917, and June 30, 1915, VER.

Pigeonblood Ruby

135

PIGEONBLOOD RUBY: This chapter on Tosh appears to have been added to the manuscript after it was typed. The chapter on S. W. Straus & Company (changed by Altemus to "Struber & Company") ends on page 160, and page 161 begins a chapter on Fred F. French & Co. (changed by Altemus to "John J. Sinch"). The chapter on Tosh is numbered 160-a through 160-q.

135

TOSH HAD WORKED VERY HARD: Tosh bears some resemblance to Harry Winston, who established the Premier Diamond Company, with a small office on Fifth Avenue, in 1920. He built his business by purchasing rare jewels through estate sales, and then reselling or redesigning them. His company brokered the estate jewels of Arabella Huntington, widow of railroad magnate Collis P. Huntington; Emma T. Gary, widow of U.S. Steel Chairman of the Board Judge Elbert Gary (who also was a very close family friend of the Deerings); and Evalyn Walsh McLean, owner of the famed Hope Diamond, which during its long history had been purchased by a Turkish sultan (the Hope Diamond is now housed at the Smithsonian Institution, where Winston donated it in 1958). Other rare stones he owned were the Jonker, the Vargas, and the Star of the East diamonds. He also purchased rough-cut stones and crafted them into fine jewels, and loaned rare, valuable jewels to Hollywood stars for high-profile appearances. Lillian Ross, "The Big Stone: A Profile of Harry Winston: I," *New Yorker Magazine*, May 8, 1954, 36–69; Ross, "The Big Stone: A Profile of Harry Winston: II," *New Yorker Magazine*, May 15, 1954, 44–73; and Laurence S. Krashes, "Harry Winston: A Story Told in Diamonds," *Gems and Gemology*, Spring 1983, 21–29.

137

HE LEFT THE OFFICE IN MAIDEN LANE: Christopher Gray, "An Unshowy Setting for Gems," *New York Times*, August 29, 2008.

139

IT IS TITANIA'S BIRTHDAY: George F. Kunz, *The Curious Lure of Precious Stones* (Philadelphia: J. B. Lippincott, 1913); Glenn Klein, *Faceting History: Cutting Diamonds and Colored Stones* (Xlibris, 2005), 207–9; and Victoria Gomelsky, "Rubies, Blood-Red Beauty," *New York Times*, March 17, 2015.

143

THEY WERE A STRANGE ASSEMBLY: High-priced brothels, run by "madams" who often were former prostitutes, provided fine food, expensive wine, and extravagant furnishings for their wealthy and often politically powerful male clients. Altemus's almost naive depiction of the encounters she had there suggests that she may have been trying to impress upon her readers the dangers of being a single woman in the city.

John J. Sinch & Co.

148

JOHN J. SINCH: "John J. Sinch" was real estate developer and builder Frederick Fillmore French. He established the Fred F. French Companies in New York in 1908 and developed the "French Plan" for financing building construction by selling stock to investors instead of seeking out large bank loans. In 1920, he constructed his first office building on the corner of Forty-First Street and Madison Avenue, a sixteen-story office building where he moved his operations. French developed some of the largest building projects in New York in the 1920s and 1930s, including the Fred French Building at 551 Fifth Avenue (1927), Tudor City (1927-30), the largest housing project ever undertaken in Manhattan, and Knickerbocker Village (1933). He also built the Hotel Everglades in Miami in 1925, one of the tallest buildings in the city at the time. Donald L. Miller, *Supreme City: How Jazz Age Manhattan Gave Birth to Modern America* (New York: Simon & Schuster, 2014), 216-30; Eric P. Nash, *Manhattan Skyscrapers* (New York: Princeton Architectural Press, 1999), 43; "Hotel Everglades Ad," *New York Times*, October 5, 1926; "Fred F. French Dies Suddenly Up-State," *New York Times*, August 31, 1936; and Christopher Gray, "Refurbishing Mesopotamia," *New York Times*, May 24, 1992.

148

THE ARCHITECT FOR THE COMPANY: Christopher Gray, "Refurbishing Mesopotamia"; Miller, *Supreme City*, 228.

Miami

151

I FOUND SECRETARYSHIP: The Barnaby Agency had offices on Madison Avenue in New York, the Fisher Building on Miami Beach, and the Laidlaw Building in Coral Gables. In the January 1926 issue of *Country Life Magazine*, the Barnaby Agency, along with Carl Fisher, advertised its new cooperative apartments, Villa Biscayne, that were to be built just south of La Gorce Island. In addition, the agency bought land to develop on Bird Road just west of Coral Gables. *Miami Tribune*, September 21, 1924; *New York Times*, September 6, 1924; and Villa Biscayne ad, *Country Life*, January 1926.

153

NO ONE, BOSSES, SELLERS OR BUYERS: Miami was booming in 1925, and real estate was being hawked in the streets of the city and at train stations by so-called binder boys, salesmen who would take out a binder on the purchase of a property by putting 10 percent down and then having to pay the remainder in thirty days. Yet the binder boys would then resell the binder to a higher bidder, so that the price of the property would rise since the new purchaser could resell the binder for a higher price. This practice led to frenzied real estate speculation throughout the city and created the first real estate bubble in Miami's history, a process that would come to define Miami development until the present day. Helen Muir, *Miami, USA* (Gainesville: University Press of Florida, 2000); William Drye, *American Paradise: How Our Nation Was Sold an Impossible Dream in Florida* (Lyons Press, 2015), 99–100; Henry Knight, *Tropic of Hopes: California, Florida, and the Selling of American Paradise* (Gainesville: University Press of Florida, 2013), 172–88; and Jan Nijman, *Miami: Mistress of the Americas* (Philadelphia: University of Pennsylvania Press, 2011), 23–30.

Biscayne Bay

155

"THE REAL MCCOY": Born in Syracuse, New York, William Frederick "Bill" McCoy attended the Pennsylvania Nautical School and then served on board a schooner stationed in Havana, Cuba, when the U.S.S. *Maine* exploded and set off the Spanish-American War. Soon thereafter, his family moved to Florida, and he and his brother, Ben, opened a boat service and yacht building company. The boat business soon struggled, though, and the brothers moved to Gloucester, Massachusetts, and bought several schooners to transport rum from Jamaica and the Bahamas to the East Coast after the passage of the Volstead Act of 1920. He was known as one of the leading rumrunners in America, and because his liquor was always pure and undiluted, people began referring to his product, or any product that was authentic, as "the real McCoy." He was arrested in November of 1923 when the U.S. Coast Guard seized his schooner, the *Arethusa*, which was stocked with liquor ready for delivery. McCoy pled guilty with the understanding that the indictment would be dismissed with a fine, but the federal government was adamant that he serve jail time. He was sentenced to nine months in prison before being released on Christmas Eve, 1925. He then moved back to Florida, where, he explained, "[M]y brother Ben and I have gone back to our old trade of shipbuilding, and there we are going to stay." "Sea Rumrunner Held on 2 Liquor Charges," *New York Times*, November 27, 1923; Frederic F. Van de Water, *The Real McCoy* (Garden City, NY: Doubleday, Doran & Co., 1931), 3.

156

IN CONCLUSION: Altemus's manuscript likely was written in 1932 given that the McCoy story was published in 1931 and, at the time of the writing, Prohibition still was in effect (it was repealed in 1933). In addition, her address in 1932 is 63 Southeast Sixth Street. *Polk's Miami City Directory* (Jacksonville, FL: R. L. Polk & Co., 1932).

Afterword

1. Many of the situations and stories in Altemus's manuscript echo those chronicled in secondary literature on the homosocial worlds of working women, including Susan Porter Benson, *Counter Cultures: Saleswomen, Managers, and Customers in American Department Stores, 1890–1940* (Urbana: University of Illinois Press, 1986); Joanne J. Meyerowitz, *Women Adrift: Independent Wage Earners in Chicago, 1880–1930* (Chicago: University of Chicago Press, 1988); Kathy Peiss, *Cheap Amusements: Working Women and Leisure in Turn-of-the-Century New York* (Philadelphia: Temple University Press, 1986); and Christine Stansell, *American Moderns: Bohemian New York and the Creation of a New Century* (New York: Metropolitan Books, 2000).

2. The *American Weekly* article with Altemus's annotations was included with the original manuscript when it was donated to Vizcaya by Altemus's grandsons.

3. "Illinois Births and Christenings, 1824–1940," index, *FamilySearch* (https://familysearch.org/pal:/MM9.1.1/V22N-BJ9: accessed June 27, 2014), Althea Maggie McDowell, December 4, 1885; Birth, citing Woodstock, McHenry, Illinois; FHL microfilm 1420735. "Birth Announcement," *Daily News,* December 9, 1885; *Every Saturday,* December 12, 1885; Ann Durkin Keating, *Chicagoland: City and Suburbs in the Railroad Age* (Chicago: University of Chicago Press, 2005), 43, 58. Interestingly, Orson Welles attended prep school there, at the Todd School for Boys, graduating in 1931, and staged a summer theater festival at the historic Woodstock Opera House in 1934. *Chicago Tribune,* December 5, 2008.

4. "Illinois, County Marriages, 1810–1934," index, *FamilySearch* (https://familysearch.org/pal:/MM9.1.1/KFLL-NNQ: accessed May 23, 2014), Charles J. Mcdowell and Emma M. Pierce, December 14, 1882; citing Kane, Illinois; FHL microfilm 1481108. *Holland's Elgin City Directory* (1881); *The Elgin Directory* (1885); *Directory of the City of Elgin* (1889–90); *The Watch Word* 2, no. 11 (June 1923): 12; Death records in Elgin, Illinois [vol. 1, part 2]: with burials at Bluff City Cemetery and elsewhere as re-

corded in the cemetery sextons' ledgers/coordinated by the City of Elgin Heritage Commission.

5. *Directory of the City of Elgin* (1903, 1905-6, 1907-8); *Lakeside City Directory of Chicago* (Chicago: Chicago Directory Company, 1908).

6. See Jerome P. Bjelopera, *City of Clerks: Office and Sales Workers in Philadelphia, 1870-1920* (Urbana: University of Illinois Press, 2005); Margery W. Davies, *Woman's Place Is at the Typewriter: Office Work and Office Workers, 1870-1930* (Philadelphia: Temple University Press, 1982), 51-65; Lisa M. Fine, *The Souls of the Skyscraper: Female Clerical Workers in Chicago, 1870-1930* (Philadelphia: Temple University Press, 1990); Angel Kwolek-Folland, *Engendering Business: Men and Women in the Corporate Office, 1870-1930* (Baltimore: Johns Hopkins University Press, 1994), 25; and Sharon Hartman Strom, *Beyond the Typewriter: Gender, Class, and the Origins of Modern American Office Work, 1900-1930* (Urbana: University of Illinois Press, 1992).

7. Claudia Goldin, *Understanding the Gender Gap: An Economic History of American Women* (New York: Oxford University Press, 1990), 106-7; Aimee Buchanan, *This Lady Means Business: How to Reach the Top in the Business World—the Career Woman's Own Machiavelli* (New York: Simon and Schuster, 1942), 108-13; and Kwolek-Folland, *Engendering Business*, 4.

8. Elyce Jean Rotella, "Women's Labor Force Participation and the Growth of Clerical Employment in the United States, 1870-1930" (Ph.D. diss., University of Pennsylvania, 1977), 245.

9. Janet Hooks, *Women's Occupations through Seven Decades*, Women's Bureau Bulletin no. 218 (Washington, DC: U.S. Department of Labor, 1947), 39, cited in Barbara Meyer Wertheimer, *We Were There: The Story of Working Women in America* (New York: Pantheon Books, 1977), 210.

10. Death records in Elgin, Illinois [vol. 1, part 2]: with burials at Bluff City Cemetery and elsewhere as recorded in the cemetery sextons' ledgers/coordinated by the City of Elgin Heritage Commission.

11. Census on Free Inhabitants of Philadelphia, in the County of Philadelphia, State of Pennsylvania (1850, 1860, 1880); *City Directory of Philadelphia* (1862, 1870, 1881), from Ancestry.com, *U.S. City Directories, 1822-1995* [database online], Provo, UT: Ancestry.com Operations, Inc., 2011. Eleanor Ward Altemus, "History of the Descendents [*sic*] of Johann Friederich Althomus Known in America as Frederick Altemus" (1987), typescript provided to author by Donald Altemus, housed at Vizcaya Museum and Gardens Archives. At this time, Wayne's maternal grandmother, Mary Ann Levy, was living next door with her daughter Annie Levy Childs and her son-in-law, Lyman Beecher Childs, half brother of Adelaide Childs Frick.

12. *Philadelphia City Directory* (1901); *City Directory of Philadelphia* (1862, 1870, 1881), from Ancestry.com, *U.S. City Directories, 1822-1995* [database online], Provo, UT: Ancestry.com Operations, Inc., 2011. *Lakeside City Directory of Chicago* (1905, 1906 1908, 1909); Year: *1900;* Census Place: *Philadelphia Ward 27, Philadelphia, Pennsylvania;* Roll: *1469;* Page: *9A;* Enumeration District: 0660; FHL microfilm: *1241469;* Year: *1910;* Census Place: *Philadelphia Ward 27, Philadelphia, Pennsylvania;* Roll: *T624_1401;* Page: *9A;* Enumeration District: 0620; FHL microfilm: *1375414,* from Ancestry.com.

13. Ancestry.com. *Philadelphia, Pennsylvania, Death Certificates Index, 1803-1915* [database online]. Provo, UT: Ancestry.com Operations, Inc., 2011; Thirteenth Census of the United States, Philadelphia, Pennsylvania, 1910; Woodlands Cemetery Lot Card for Section CC, Lot 51, for Altemus Family Mausoleum, Woodlands Cemetery, Philadelphia, Pennsylvania.

14. *Altemus v. Altemus,* affidavit of nonresidence, Summons in Chancery, Superior Court of Cook County, October 1916; *Altemus v. Altemus,* Bill of Complaint, Superior Court of Cook County, October 1916.

15. *Altemus v. Altemus,* Certificate of Evidence, Superior Court of Cook County, June 2, 1917; *Altemus v. Altemus,* Decree for Divorce, Superior Court of Cook County, June 17, 1917, decree no. 324560; Wayne Hughes Altemus, Draft Registration card, September 12, 1918; Ancestry.com, *U.S., WWI Civilian Draft Registrations, 1917-1918* [database online], Provo, UT: Ancestry.com Operations, Inc., 2000. Historical Society of Pennsylvania; Philadelphia, Pennsylvania; Collection Name: *Historic Pennsylvania Church and Town Records;* from Ancestry.com, *Pennsylvania, Oliver H. Bair Funeral Records Indexes, 1920-1980* [database online], Provo, UT: Ancestry.com Operations, Inc., 2012. *New York Times,* August 25, 1922.

16. James Deering to Paul Chalfin, November 12, 1917, Vizcaya Estate Records, Series 1: Correspondence, Vizcaya Museum and Gardens Archives, hereafter cited as VER.

17. Minnie B. Trapp, *My Pioneer Reminiscences,* 1941; Special Collections, University of Miami Libraries.

18. G. L. Miller & Co., "Miami—Some Reasons Why" (Miami, FL: Hefty Press, 1917), Special Collections, Otto G. Richter Library, University of Miami.

19. Mark S. Foster, *Castles in the Sand: The Life and Times of Carl Graham Fisher* (Gainesville: University Press of Florida, 2000), 44, 55, 75-79; Howard Kleinberg, *Miami Beach: A History* (Miami, FL: Centennial Press, 1994), 27-36; J. N. Lummus, *The Miracle of Miami Beach* (Miami, FL: Miami Post Publishing Company, 1952); Helen Muir, *Miami, U.S.A.* (1953; reprinted, Miami, FL: Pickering Press, 1990); Polly Redford, *Billion-Dollar Sandbar:*

A Biography of Miami Beach (New York: E. P. Dutton and Co., 1970), 54–64; and F. Page Wilson, *Miami, from Frontier to Metropolis* (Miami: Historical Association of Southern Florida, 1956), 27–28.

20. F. Burrall Hoffman Jr. and Paul Chalfin, "Vizcaya, the Villa and Grounds: A House at Miami, Florida," *Architectural Review* 5, no. 7 (July 1917): 121.

21. *Handbook of the House, Formal Gardens and Fountains of Vizcaya* (Miami, FL: Dade County Art Museum, 1953), 14.

22. "Income Tax Reporting," July 13, 1920, Box 37 Folder 4, VER.

23. Deering to Chalfin, October 28, 1918 and May 24, 1919, VER.

24. William Lauderback to Althea Altemus, October 18, 1917 and January 23, 1918, VER; Althea Altemus to William Lauderback, October 23, 1917, VER.

25. *Polk & Co.'s Miami City Directory* (Jacksonville, FL: R. L. Polk & Co., 1920, 1921, 1922); *1920 United States Federal Census: Miami, Dade, Florida;* Roll: *T625_216;* Page: *2A;* Enumeration District: *31;* Image: *455.* "Issues Fifteen More Permits, 2 Days," *Miami Herald,* November 9, 1920; "Legal Notices," *Miami Herald,* July 22, 1922.

26. Althea Altemus, "Big Bosses," 124–25.

27. Altemus, "Big Bosses," 133.

28. See Davies, *Woman's Place Is at the Typewriter,* 79–96; Lisa M. Fine, *The Souls of the Skyscraper,* 31–34, 51–54, 96–103; Strom, *Beyond the Typewriter,* 8, 190–96, 388; and Lynn Y. Weiner, *From Working Girl to Working Mother: The Female Labor Force in the United States* (Chapel Hill: University of North Carolina Press, 1985), 98–110.

29. See Meyerowitz, *Women Adrift;* Ruth Rosen, *The Lost Sisterhood: Prostitution in America, 1900–1908* (Baltimore: Johns Hopkins University Press, 1982); and Timothy J. Gilfoyle, *City of Eros: New York City, Prostitution, and the Commercialization of Sex, 1790–1920* (New York: W. W. Norton & Co., 1994).

30. Kenneth Roberts, "Florida Loafing," *Saturday Evening Post,* May 17, 1924, quoted in Arva Moore Parks, *George Merrick, Son of the South Wind: Visionary Creator of Coral Gables* (Gainesville: University Press of Florida, 2015), 196.

31. *Miami Tribune,* September 21, 1924; *New York Times,* September 6, 1924; Villa Biscayne ad, *Country Life,* January, 1926; Ancestry.com. *U.S. Public Records Index, 1950–1993, Volume 2* [database online]. Provo, UT: Ancestry.com Operations, Inc., 2010.

32. 1940 U.S. Federal Census: *Miami, Dade, Florida;* Roll: *T627_631;* Page: *1A;* Enumeration District: *69-87B; Polk & Co.'s Miami City Directory* (Jacksonville, FL: R. L. Polk & Co., 1935, 1938, 1940, 1942).

33. *Polk & Co.'s Miami City Directory* (Jacksonville, FL: R. L. Polk & Co., 1935, 1938, 1940, 1942); 1930 U.S. Federal Census: *Miami, Dade, Florida;* Roll: *311;* Page: *4A;* Enumeration District: 0071; Image: *173.0;* FHL microfilm: *2340046;* 1940 U.S. Federal Census: *Miami, Dade, Florida;* Roll: *T627_631;* Page: *1A;* Enumeration District: *69-87B.* "Robert Altemus Handwritten Interview Notes," Vizcaya Museum and Gardens Archives; and Oral History Interview, "Don Altemus Interviewed by Robin Bachin and Recorded by Emily Gibson," June 10, 2015, Collection ID: RG010/001, Vizcaya Museum and Gardens Archives.

34. "Leonard L. Abess, Sr. Obituary," *Florida Sun-Sentinel,* June 6, 2001; *Polk & Co.'s Miami City Directory* (Jacksonville, FL: R. L. Polk & Co., 1940, 1942, 1945, 1947, 1949, 1953, 1955, 1959, 1966); Year: *1940;* Census Place: *Miami, Dade, Florida;* Roll: *T627_628;* Page: *12A;* Enumeration District: *69-15C.*

35. "Robert Altemus Handwritten Interview Notes," Vizcaya Museum and Gardens Archives; Oral History Interview, "Don Altemus"; "Miami Stories: Don Altemus, Pinecrest, FL," *Miami Herald,* June 3, 2014; and Conversation between Robin Bachin and Tanya Lewicki, July 6, 2015.

36. "Robert Altemus Handwritten Interview Notes," Vizcaya Museum and Gardens Archives. The Altemus family connection to Vizcaya has continued, for in 2015, Althea's great-granddaughter, Dona Marie Altemus, participated in the Vizcaya Contemporary Arts Program's "Fantastical Vizcaya," a project featuring eleven local artists who created site-specific installations at the estate in conjunction with Art Basel Miami Beach. "Vizcaya's Contemporary Art Program Highlights Local Artists during Art Basel," http://vizcaya.org/library/press-releases/2015-11-05-vizcaya-contemporary-arts.pdf.

37. Bureau of Vital Statistics, State of Florida, Certificate of Death, Althea Marie Altemus, aka Marie, State File Number 65-028275, June 21, 1965; "Marie M. Altemus: Death Notice," *Miami Herald,* June 22, 1965.

38. See Jan Cohn, *Creating America: George Horace Lorimer and the Saturday Evening Post* (Pittsburgh: University of Pittsburgh Press, 1989); Helen Damon-Moore, *Magazines for the Millions: Gender and Commerce in the Ladies' Home Journal and the Saturday Evening Post, 1880–1910* (Albany: State University of New York Press, 1994); and Janice Radway, *Reading the Romance: Women, Patriarchy, and Popular Literature* (Chapel Hill: University of North Carolina Press, 1994).